Pivotal Moments 101 Real Stories, Real Women, Real Lives

Voices of Courage

BRENDA DEMPSEY

BALBOA.
PRESS
A DIVISION OF HAY HOUSE

Balboa Press books may be ordered through booksellers or by contacting:

Balboa Press
A Division of Hay House
1663 Liberty Drive
Bloomington, IN 47403
www.balboapress.com
1 (877) 407-4847

Because of the dynamic nature of the Internet, any web addresses or links contained in this book may have changed since publication and may no longer be valid. The views expressed in this work are solely those of the author and do not necessarily reflect the views of the publisher, and the publisher hereby disclaims any responsibility for them.

The author of this book does not dispense medical advice or prescribe the use of any technique as a form of treatment for physical, emotional, or medical problems without the advice of a physician, either directly or indirectly. The intent of the author is only to offer information of a general nature to help you in your quest for emotional and spiritual well-being. In the event you use any of the information in this book for yourself, which is your constitutional right, the author and the publisher assume no responsibility for your actions.

Any people depicted in stock imagery provided by Thinkstock are models, and such images are being used for illustrative purposes only. Certain stock imagery © Thinkstock.

Print information available on the last page.

ISBN: 978-1-5043-9220-4 (sc)
ISBN: 978-1-5043-9221-1 (hc)
ISBN: 978-1-5043-9366-9 (e)

Library of Congress Control Number: 2017918465

Balboa Press rev. date: 02/13/2018

FOREWORD

 Challenges: they are here to strengthen our character, weaken our fears and bring to the forefront the woman we are meant to be: a powerful leader and a bright beam of light for thousands, even millions, of others.

The collection of stories in Brenda's anthology, Pivotal Moments 101, is an incredible insight into the many struggles women face – and successfully overcome - in their lifetimes. Each story brings out so many wonderful (and wonderfully different) attributes of the human spirit, which often show themselves especially at the lowest points in your life, during challenges that – as illustrated masterfully – lead to the rapid and long-lasting transformations which you desire.

I thank Brenda's inner genius for bringing these stories, and the women from around the world behind them, together. They collectively show us how a woman's strength, courage and determination to change create a powerful and hopeful message for others. These women dared to raise their voice and share their vulnerable stories so that you can do so too and further drive the change in the world.

Raising your Voice as a Woman is a shared duty and privilege that we ought not to take lightly, but embrace fully. Because when we do, we, as women individually, and the world, only can change in the most magical of ways.

Impacting the world is the journey ahead of you, starting from chapter one of this anthology, finishing with the legacy you leave for this world. Enjoy!

LENKA LUTONSKA BUSINESS STRATEGIST AND MINDSET MAVEN FOR WOMEN COACHES AND CHANGE-MAKERS WWW. LENKALUTONSKA.COM

LOVE FOR PIVOTAL MOMENTS 101

"Inside of this book, the honesty is undeniable. Story-telling truly is the best way to heal any wounds inside that have thus far, been unexplainable. Each story allows the reader to connect deeply with the writer, in the heart space of love".

Carla Wynn Hall, Best Selling Author, "The Soul Code" www.carlawynnhall.com

"Pivotal Moments 101 is a collection of work written by real women with real lives. The stories are moving, sad and inspirational — all different situations with authors from various countries. I am sure this book will help a great many women."

STEPHANIE HALE, AUTHOR 'MILLIONAIRE WOMEN, MILLIONAIRE YOU" http://www.stephaniejhale.com/

Pivotal Moments is a document of women, their vulnerabilities, challenges and ultimately their triumphs. It is a thought-provoking, inspiring and motivating read that reminds us all, men and women, that we are not alone in our fears, anxieties and seemingly insurmountable obstacles. We all encounter them just not perhaps at the same time. These are women not looking for pity or admiration but seeking to create empathy with others feeling lost, defeated and isolated. It is a reminder for us to strive to be the best version of ourselves. Incredible stories beautifully told."

YVONNE JOYE, FREELANCE JOURNALIST AND AUTHOR

What a beauty-full collection of stories, I laughed, I cried, felt empathy and admiration. As I navigate a difficult time in my own life, it's both reassuring and inspiring to read stories of amazing women who have blossomed through life's adversity.

SARAH McCASKEY, YOGA TEACHER
www.yourspace-online.co.uk

Brenda Dempsey has done a fantastic job in compiling these heart-touching stories of women. We are our stories, and one woman's story is every woman's story! I am deeply touched by their life-changing moments and how they chose to rise above the adversities. These stories will leave you with a spark of hope, courage and self-compassion and assist you in defining your pivotal moments. I also loved the inclusion of poetry and visual arts as they are crucial expressions in the rising feminine consciousness. These voices of courage will take you on a journey of embracing your life's challenges with an attitude of gratitude.

JONITA D'SOUZA. FEMININE LIFESTYLIST, AUTHOR & CREATRESS OF EXPLORING FEMININITY
http://jonitadsouza.com

Well done Brenda Dempsey, at last a genuinely impressive book about real women which will motivate and inspire. Life deals some horrendous cards but reading how these ladies turn 'accidents' into purpose is very moving. Love the quotes. I will pick this book up again and again.

MARY FLAVELLE Co-Founder Ladies Who Latte

Pivotal Moments 101, is a brilliant collection of real stories by real women with real lives, created by Brenda Dempsey. It speaks to the soul of the individual and the collective. Our stories so often define us, there is a magic when we free ourselves from the past and empower others through sharing the gifts of our lessons. Bringing our truth gives permission to heal and create something new with our wisdom. May this book bring you comfort and joy knowing you are one of many who walks this road of life. You are strong and delicate, you are a phoenix rising.

LACEY ESHLEMAN, IGNITE CONSCIOUSNESS COACH, ARTIST, ALCHEMIST OF LIFE.

RESURGE EX CINERIBUS

For the Love of Pat
1950 - 2016

RESURGE EX CINERIBUS

Contents

Prologue xv

Transformation #1   Finding My Purpose 1
                     Louize Spittle

Transformation #2   From the Dark to the Light........................... 5
                     Dovile Strazdiene

Transformation #3   The Power of Choice 10
                     Gitana Shillin

Transformation #4   A Journey of Re-Birth................................. 14
                     Lauren Hornby

Transformation #5   From Comfort Zone to Confidence Zone..... 18
                     Trina Kavanagh

Transformation #6   Awakened and Walking in Wisdom............. 23
                     Willow Sterrick

Transformation #7   A Path to Power 28
                     Anita Smith

Transformation #8   Reality is Negotiable 32
                     Bonnie Harmon

Transformation #9   When the Darkness Lifts 38
                     Kate Young

Transformation #10   Enjoying the Food Twice 43
                     Orit Adiri

Transformation #11   Life's Disasters bear Great Gifts 49
                      Fiona Clark

Transformation #12   Fear, Friendship and Faith 53
                      Alison Watson

Transformation #13   Call of the Soul 58
                      Samara Jacobs

Transformation #14   Passing the Test 62
                      Carey Boyce

Transformation #15   An Act of Self-Acceptance 67
                      Theresa Fowler

Transformation #16   A New Year - A New Beginning 71
                      Natalie Bird

Transformation #17   Life – A Bumpy Ride! 76
                      Annie Heggie

Transformation #18   Vulnerability 80
                      Samara Jacobs

Transformation #19   Going with My Gut 82
                      Alison Fennell

Transformation #20   Fate Creates a Better Life 86
                      Zeleen Teter

Transformation #21   You be you, I'll be me and together,
                      let's be us 91
                      Bethany Rivett-Carnac

Transformation #22   Becoming Elizabeth 96
                      Elizabeth Carney

Transformation #23   Awakened Courage 101

Emma Stuart

Transformation #24   Acceptance 106
                      Sarah Rossellini

Transformation #25   A Journey to Teheran, a Personal Story
                      in a Historical Context 111
                      Amira Ben Mor

Transformation #26   Gratitude for Life 117
                      Roslyn Bell

Transformation #27   Finding Me 122
                      Barbara Byrne

Transformation #28   When the Universe Showed Me the Way ... 126
                      Lucy Tobias

Transformation #29   Breaking Open 132
                      Erron Noel

Transformation #30   Forgiveness Means Letting Go 138
                      Debbie Arthurs

Transformation #31   The Power of Decisions 143
                      Jurgita Kasparr

Transformation #32   Everything is possible............................... 148
                      Rita Grineviciene

Transformation #33   The Darkest Hour is just Before Dawn 155
                      Brenda Dempsey

Epilogue.. 159
Acknowledgements 163
Meet Co-Authors 165
About the Creator 179

Prologue

When you face a challenge in life, you often feel isolated, afraid and paralysed. You become so introverted that everything, while desperate, is magnified and you unconsciously punish yourself by holding silence.

You face a diminishing spiral of hopelessness. Consciously your self-esteem, self-worth and value are eroded by the spurious thoughts that relentlessly run through your mind. The darkness descends until you feel the oppression of blackness.

When you add time into the mix, your magnified feelings of wretchedness become overbearing, and you may enter a zone of numbness in protection against collateral damage to your soul.

I found myself in such a place on more than one occasion in my life. I know you will have too.

Hardship, emotional tornados and familiar situations are just some of the key ingredients that bind us together. When you dare to put your face over the parapet, you can see some light and a single dark shadow. You begin to think, "Maybe they can help me?"

Questioning is the seed of hope. You start to think, "I'm not alone after all." Next, comes the dialogue within your head. "What can I do?" "How can I leave?" "Who can I trust to help me?" Then you think the killer of hope, if you let it. "What will people think of me?"

I am sure these thoughts and a thousand more have run through your mind when confronted with what you once determined as an insurmountable challenge. Whether faced with abuse, self-loathing or unfulfillment in life, you unconsciously allowed them to keep you returning for more of the same.

What do you say to yourself when you've had enough?

I use the term, "Enough, is enough, is enough!" You may say something similar to, "I'm done" or "Enough is Enough" or "That's it, I'm out of here!" Whatever the words that are yours, you come to the point of no return. It's time to change, be released from your situation and take control.

These phrases mark your PIVOTAL MOMENT.

A Pivotal Moment is a 'turning point in time'. A turning point when you make a decision like no other decision ever made. Why? It comes from the depth of your soul. It's a decision that spurs you on no matter what. It's a decision that has you looking at your challenge in a different and transformational way. It's a decision that will change you and your life forever.

Pivotal Moments bring hope, clarity and light. They unlock your paralysis; unveil your voice and unleash a latent power within. I like to call this your Inner Diamond Power. You see, you have been in the dark, yes. You have endured incredible pressure, yes. You awaken the indestructible rough diamond that has potential to be brilliant, strong and unique.

Pivotal Moments reveal resilience, strength and courage. You have a vision that you keep in your mind's eye no matter what. You have unleashed your incredible WHY and nothing will stop you from achieving your goal.

I have learned this from the many pivotal moments in my life, and there's more...

With the acceptance of your Pivotal Moment, it gives you courage, strength and a common bond in which to connect with other women. Within this connection, you experience a sisterhood, in knowing that you can achieve more in unison than alone. Understanding, knowing and soul connections bind us together as one.

My mission is to assist women in being the best version of them, living in super consciousness and manifesting their dreams whatever they may be. One approach I have learned to do this is through giving women courage, belief and confidence to raise their voices so they can share their stories, both in writing and speaking.

You all know the power of stories. Since time began, stories have been a vehicle for connecting us at a deeper level than mere words.

[1]A neuroscience study explained why telling stories builds empathy, brain synchronicity and people act as if they›re watching it unfold before them. We love human stories.

It is my vision to connect women from around the world. In finding a common bond more than simply being a woman yet as women know the real power of our feminine essence and energy. Embracing this Divine Feminine Energy uplifts us and the world in which we live. Joining in its harmony generates a powerful energy that creates change for the better within us and others.

For these reasons and more I have been the vessel of the creation of this book, Pivotal Moments 101.

By giving a platform for the Real Women, their Real Stories and revealing their Real Lives it has produced a place of healing, acceptance and of letting go.

I am humbled and privileged by all the brave, bold and beautiful women who said, "YES" to being part of, Pivotal Moments 101, Volume 1: Voices of Courage. They are re-energised, excited and hopeful for their futures. They illustrate their strength, courage and transformation through their experiences and I know that when you read them, you too will feel the power of their unique stories bringing renewed hope to you and others.

Be Empowered
Be Brilliant & Sparkle
Brenda Dempsey

[1]https://www.psychologytoday.com/blog/you-illuminated/201106/why-sharing-stories-brings-people-together?collection=67103

RESURGE EX CINERIBUS

The Art of Feminine Beauty

Up in the Highlands
By
Patricia Dempsey

Up in the highlands where the air is clear,
The blackness of night holds a secret so dear;
So look to the heavens, the northern sky bright;
A million stars twinkle as they switch on the light.

There, beauty is a dream for just a few
So don't go telling or there will be a queue.
This land so peaceful, nothing stirs;
Simply nature and me in this forest of firs.

The early bird song, calls a new day.
The buzzard circles looking for prey.
The flowing river meanders on by.
The angels sing from on high

When darkness falls and the moon smiles
The silence expands for miles and miles
And in the quiet of this wondrous night
A choir so pure, voice their delight

RESURGE EX CINERIBUS

Transformation #1

Finding My Purpose

*"That which does not **kill** us **makes** us **stronger**."*

Friedrich Nietzsche

As I sit here, writing about a pivotal moment in my recent past, I am going through another pivotal moment right now. You see life is full of them. Some of those moments are more pivotal than the other! (That story will be for another time though) This story is one of strength, determination, bravery and courage at a time I felt myself crumbling to pieces.

It was January 2016, and my daughter Elsie was just three months old and my son almost four years old. It was cold and wet outside, and inside I had dirty nappies, bottles to make and a preschooler who also needed attention. I had reached ground hog day and was desperate for change. I was fed up of the thankless tasks that I would do all day every day, picking up toys and vacuuming just for the mess to return when you enter the room again about thirty seconds later. Everything became a chore to me, and I hit an all-time low. The demands on me were overbearing, and I was single handed doing it all while my partner was busy at work earning money to keep a roof over our heads.

All I wanted was to be able to snuggle up with my babies and enjoy our time together. Instead, I felt like they were stressing me out!!

To say I was finding it hard being a mom for the second time is an understatement. You see for years before this I had been on and off anti-depressants due to depression and stress for various reasons. Now I felt I had hit an all-time low point when I should have been enjoying being a mom; you know like all those other moms portray it to be!

Anyway, I felt myself sliding down a familiar slippery slope and reached out in the only way I knew how by reaching out to the National Health Service (NHS). They offered me help with antidepressants which I turned down. I had been on, and off them previously due to Post Traumatic Stress Disorder, Depression and Post Natal Depression and I could recognise the same old cycle that I was repeating.

This time I wanted something more, something that would drastically change the way I felt instead of just masking over the problem yet again. It had to be something I could do for myself and also be able to use again should the need arise in the future.

That was when I heard about Neuro Linguistic Programming (NLP). A friend told me she was going to be attending a free coaching weekend and when I did my research it seemed to be everything I had been searching! I picked up the phone and spoke to the course trainers, and I discovered that the free weekend on offer would be the perfect introduction to Neuro Linguistic Programming.

I went along to the free coaching weekend. It was exciting, and I enjoyed it so much that I signed up to train as a Practitioner of NLP, Practitioner of Hypnotherapy, Practitioner of Time Line Therapy and also an NLP Coach.

You know about the proverbial bubble? Well, mine just burst. Despite my excitement at starting my course, my emotions held me in a vice. I thought things couldn't get any worse. I became rather withdrawn and emotional, and my Health Visitor referred me to a Mother and Baby Mental Health Unit. I went along scared at the possibility that they may take my beautiful children from me or lock me in the Unit with them and give me anti-depressants. I went along nervously and saw a Consultant who listened carefully to my plan of attending the course to become a Practitioner of Neuro Linguistic Programming, Practitioner of Hypnotherapy, Practitioner of Time Line Therapy and also an NLP Coach. The Consultant smiled at me and told me I should go and attend the course as it would be much more beneficial to me than being admitted to the Mother and Baby Unit.

June 2016 rolled around, and I participated in the course and became certified as a Practitioner of Neuro Linguistic Programming, Practitioner of Hypnotherapy, Practitioner of Time Line Therapy and also an NLP Coach. During the course, I met many new people, and I grew so much as a person; my confidence grew hugely, and I gained belief in myself. I enjoyed it so much I went on to book the next step of becoming a Master Practitioner of Neuro linguistic programming, Master Practitioner of Hypnotherapy, Master Practitioner of Time Line Therapy and also a Master NLP Coach in the November 2016.

During the course I had to go through the therapy and coaching myself, ridding negative emotion from past events and putting new strategies into place. The positive physical and mental change I made by releasing these negative emotions are transforming and liberating! Following this, I radiated happiness and glowed from within for what felt like the first time in a long time. On the last day of our Master's training, I turned 30 years old. I left my NHS job and set up my Coaching and Therapy Business; an opportunity for me to shine likes a beacon of light to help others through dark stormy times. I now help other women release negative emotions that may overwhelm them and coach them in many areas of life.

All in all most people I know supported me going through this pivotal moment. Some people may attempt to knock you down along the way or even pull you back, so you never progress. One word of advice, when you get to the point that change is needed, reach out, make a plan and stick to that plan no matter what is said or done by naysayers; those who care will be by your side, cheering you along the way. So head forward, focus and only glance back to remember where you came from and how far you have come along the way.

Louize Spittle – Codsall, UK

I dedicate this chapter to my babies, Archie John Jackson Spittle and Elsie Violet Jackson Spittle. I will always be strong for you. Love Mommy xxx

RESURGE EX CINERIBUS

Transformation #2

From the Dark to the Light

"Your wings are ready."

John Assaraf

I am **Dovile Strazdiene** abstract artist, wife and mother, stage four cancer survivor. I would like to tell you my story about what I learned in 34 beautiful years of my life. My quest is to inspire and uplift others who are fighting a deadly illness or hesitating to take the first step to their dreams. Be free and light like the wind and then fight; become the tempest because after each storm comes calmness and peace. Life lessons are testing us, and when the lesson is learned, you must share your experience with others.

The first spiritual book I read was written by Louise Hay "You Can Heal Your Life." I find her painful childhood experience inspiring, as well as the fact she is a cancer survivor, best-selling author, inspirational speaker and international coach. "If you are willing to change your thinking, you can change your life," says Louise Hay, who shares her experiences and journey with self-publishing. And the **"Balboa Press"** a division of Hay House is the publisher of this book.

The power of Louise Hay's positive self-esteem affirmations helped me a great deal when cancer came unexpectedly. Whenever I had chemotherapy, I imagined that my blood was the river of love. I did not experience any severe side-effects of the drugs, except a little bit of nausea and that's it. When I started to lose my hair, my husband cut it with his beard shaving clippers. I became accustomed to being hairless very quickly. My two-year-old son touched me when he said, "MUMMY YOU ARE SO BEAUTIFUL!"

Below is an extract from my journal during my fight with cancer.

Abstract vision

In a tall tree, an orange crow was sitting. In my mouth, I still tasted yesterday's food. In the middle of the hospital ward, I saw the doctor's white smock. On the old bed corner, a red wig was hanging. Life and death are very close here. In the corridor, the most beautiful song rang out like the laughter of a child. Through the window, I saw the new green leaves on the trees; it seemed like hair flying in the wind.

In my mind, I am taking a colour palette and painting the flowers of paradise. Through my vein, the endless needles injected. I am closing my eyes and starting to imagine the river of love flowing in my blood. On the wall, a lobster crawls slowly. Night sweats enlarged lymph nodes; it's the painting of October. The black book already closed and on the wall, the calmness of Da Vinci's Mona Lisa hangs.

Conscious Decision

"Dovile, a new stage of your life is starting. You could choose to go to the cemetery or fly like a bird." Nothing in your life happens without reason. There are always reasons and the cause and effect rule. Diligently engage in daily work with yourself: healthy eating; 6 am morning run, and art therapy are the main activities I did, encouraged by those who helped me to survive my cancer.

I am the creator of my life. Intense pain causes you to search inwards, feel free to express your gifts and talents and compelled to share them with others. I am light and love, and I am sharing it with others. Life is a miracle. People's bodies and souls are unlimited; it's only ourselves who create the limits. Life is limitless. We are teachers and the owners of our life. You have to step outside of your comfort zone, take risks to create your miracle. THE MIRACLE IS IN EVERY ONE OF US!!!! YOU ARE THE MIRACLE! LOVE YOURSELF! LIFE IS BEAUTIFUL!

Dovile I LOVE YOU! I AM PROUD OF YOUR BRAVENESS AND YOUR STRENGTH! YOU ARE COMING HOME TO YOURSELF. YOUR ARE UNIQUE. YOU ARE TALENTED. YOU ARE CREATIVE. YOU ARE SHINING PEACE AND LOVE TO OTHER CREATIONS OF GOD. YOU ARE SURROUNDED BY POSITIVE PEOPLE. THEY ARE LIFTING AND INSPIRING YOU. YOU ARE THE CHILD OF THE SUN. I LOVE YOU!

Winter Spirit

It's snowing again. White light fragile snowflakes are falling to earth. No one is the same. EVERY SNOWFLAKE IS UNIQUE AND PERFECT LIKE PEOPLE. White snow was covering our beautiful world; PEACEFUL AND FEELING GOOD IN MY HEART.

It was around Christmas 2015 when told I had cancer, and this book will be in the bookstores around Christmas too. I LOVE COINCIDENCES. But you know there are no coincidences in our life, only crossed paths through awakening. The "**Awakened Soul**" is the final step- the progression of the Old **Soul** who has undergone immense spiritual work.

Enjoy every minute of your time like children. Express gratitude for everything you have. Only gratefulness doubles your treasures. Only positivity fights fear, pessimism, depression and apathy. I am happy because I AM. I came to this world with my mission to create joy!

"Love yourself."

When the ray of sun touches my eyes with its smile my morning begins. I exercise; after my morning run, I shower, then breakfast. Unconsciously the pen is in my hand, writing gratitude into my diary pages, it is uncontrollable, happily dancing on the white pages. It appears like a fantasy, but actually, you are programming your day. The kindness is flowing throughout your body.

When you experience a 'bad' day, tears, the feeling like a weighty stone on your heart, it's a signal that you're not giving enough time to yourself. Remember loving yourself is wavy like a sea, that's why you have to watch for the coming of the storm. Be in nature, ride a bike, find time to observe a plane in the sky, and seek the courage to feel zero gravity. You don't have to wait for someone to show you the way to love yourself.

Dovile Strazdiene - Vilnius, Lithuania

I dedicate this chapter to my grandmother, Ona Kulbokiene, who died of breast cancer.

The Art of Feminine Beauty

Roses of Hope by Dovile Strazdiene

This painting was born at the cosy art studio in the garden of my painting teacher Egle. I had such a pleasure to play with the colours and new techniques. This painting inspires people and makes them feel secure and powerful. Intuitive art allows you to express emotions in a secure way. My life goal is to inspire and uplift people through art and to remember their soul gifts, Full colour copy can be found at https://society6.com/product/summers-flowers577171_print#s6-7297200p4a1v45

Transformation #3

The Power of Choice

"Be yourself – everyone else is already taken."

Oscar Wilde

I was born into a family of violent and abusive relationships. Regardless of the numerous fights at home we still managed to remain a respectable family in the eyes of the community, because my Mum always hid everything from preying eyes.

I grew up, finished school, fell in love, got married and followed my Mum's footsteps.

To start with my husband had a problem with drinking but later on, it led to violence and abuse. Unfortunately, I have to admit, in time it came from both sides as I fought back. My husband's childhood was much worse than mine, and he kept saying that his family will never go through the hell he did and I believed him for a very long time. You know what? I did the same as my Mum – I hid everything as much as I could. Even my closest friends and family didn't know the real picture because I felt I was failing at my marriage and didn't want to admit it to anyone. I portrayed my husband in bright colours and prayed people would believe me. Sweet naivety – I thought I had power to change that man because, if you truly love someone you will change, right? Well, he did change but not for the better, and I changed with him.

I was living in constant struggle and worry about all aspects of my life – relationship, romance, finance, holidays (holidays? Never had them)! I applied for divorce twice and twice didn't go through with it. Why? Because I didn't have enough power to resist the pressure he was putting on me and it was just easier to give in, so I did what was easier trying to avoid an extra worry at any cost. All I wanted was a bit of love and affection and peace and quiet.

There's an excellent saying "You can't run away from yourself", and in my case, it was on point. I was running away from my problems without even realising that the problem is actually in mine. We moved from our country to England, and I was hoping that my life will miraculously change. I was distraught and depressed when I realised that the pattern of my life is repeating once again.

I came to the UK without speaking English, so I needed to learn the language and adapt to the country's way of life. Once I learnt it I was working, studying in the college, looking after the house, children, and husband (you see, he never studied the language, so it was up to me to take care of him now too). I felt exhausted, depressed, and worthless. By now I wanted to move to a deserted island so no one could find me! I felt like being pulled in different directions without my consent, without any appreciation for what I do until one day I decided – enough is enough! I don't want to live that life! I don't want to live with that man!

About a year later, we were living separate lives in the same house, and our gorgeous children stuck in the middle of all the mayhem. It was quite ironic because in this particular year I received a bunch of beautiful flowers for my birthday. That was the first time in all nineteen years of marriage that he gave me anything at all for my birthday.

That same year I met someone else and, when I told him, it all ended up with him arrested. You see, in his mind, he still had a picture of us being a perfect family, and I was the one destroying it. He thought with the bunch of flowers and a box of chocolates we could fix it all. Unfortunately, it was too little too late.

Once he'd gone, I realised that I never felt any better, to be fair, mentally I was feeling worse and worse. I was on and off medication for the most of my adult life, so I went on tablets again. Through the eyes of an outsider, it probably looked like I had a good life – I had a job, a house to live in, two children who I adore and have their unconditional love, the man who loves me and who I love back. Nevertheless, something was nagging, lurking in the corner of my mind. Something I couldn't get the grasp of; something so close but still not accessible. That was until I joined a Network Marketing Company which, to my greatest advantage was keen on self-development.

Since the day I read that first book, I feel like I discovered a whole new world that hid from me for too long. That was when it all clicked – it wasn't anyone else's fault that I was so unhappy living my life! It was me who needed to change!

The first thing I realised was that we are all responsible for our lives. How was I responsible for my husband's actions? Well, I brought that man into my life. I forgave him the first time he raised his voice or hand to me. I carried on living with him despite applying for divorce twice. I hadn't told him to go to hell when I needed! It was ME; all the way ME! I either brought everything into my life by my thoughts and actions, or I just allowed it to happen. When it all became clear, I felt such a wave of power within me.

I realised that by complaining about other people doing all the nasty stuff to me, I am giving my power away. I cannot change how other people act towards me because I haven't got the power over their actions, but I have the ability to either accept it or say, "You know what, that's not on. If you can't respect me, then I can't have you in my life." I've got A CHOICE.

Gitana Shillin – Lithuanian living in the UK

I dedicate this chapter to my children Dominyka and Gvidas. They are my WHY that kept me going all those years. They are the reason I am always searching for a better life for us. I want to give my thanks and appreciation to my partner Pete for loving me for who I am and always standing beside.

Transformation #4

A Journey of Re-Birth

"The moment you choose a new story for your life you begin the journey of transforming your greatest wounds into your greatest gifts."

After years of being lost, being taken downstream by the momentum of the stories and the thoughts that ran through my mind every day, only escaping through psychotic episodes, I found myself losing grip of reality. It was as though I was an observer in my own life, standing two feet behind my body always, watching, and going through the motions, day by day. It was monotonous and dark, and I longed for a way out, but I couldn't see one.

Like every other Tuesday night. I found myself sitting in a car park waiting for my friends, as I did before our weekly drama class. Except this night was different, my friends were running late. There was something different about that night. It was very still and quiet. The lonely darkness outside reflected my inner world. In the distance, I had followed the outline of a church with my eyes; it had been lit up by the coloured lights that surrounded it. I remember feeling numb; a familiar feeling of not being here, not being grounded. There isn't exactly a word that describes that dark place.

It was a surreal moment. I reached over into my bag and took out my psychotic medication. I took each tablet one at a time, really slowly, almost devoid of any feeling, any thought, and I just sat there staring out of the window.

I had let the abuse I experienced as a child stalk me, and it was as though I had imagined it into an entity that lurked in the background of my life and cast a dark shadow, a shadow that made the world I perceived appear dark and hopeless.

But this day, though one of my darkest marked the moment that everything changed. I had a moment of complete clarity, where something sparked inside me, a kind of power, and a determination that took over my whole body. At that moment, and the days following leaving the hospital, I remembered myself; my worth, the child who longed to be seen, to tell the truth, to be cared for, to be loved. This innate need was the part of me I had hidden away, even from those who were closest to me.

This day was the realization I did not want death but longed for escape. I yearned for life. I wanted to feel alive, present in my body and here on this earth. I'd spent my whole childhood avoiding pain and numbing myself to the outside world. However, I craved emotion, feeling, and wanted to experience the whole of me and my life. With this epiphany came a surge of energy, a life force and it was the fuel that I needed to propel me into the next chapter of my life, and that's what it did.

After this, I turned around to face the story that had led me to this moment. For so long I had lived in the shadow of my fear, hiding its secret. The moment I faced it, acknowledged the pain had held me hostage for many years, and listened to its story, it could no longer cast that shadow on my world. I could see in colour again, it has been a long and is still an ongoing journey, but it was a passage back to life again.

I continue to find my hidden gifts and embrace them on this journey of self-discovery and recovery. It has taught me how to establish healthy boundaries. I found respect for myself and others and I learned how to say 'no' to what I didn't want, but yes to my life. But the greatest gift that my experience gave me was the ability to live and sit with my pain, so that it could no longer shape my life, but rather, with the loosening grip of fear, I had the potential and the strength to change my life.

I use the gifts from this experience in my everyday life. It has strengthened my talent to work with people, families and children. Knowing that part of me so well has allowed me to be there for the children I work with; to be the person that I needed as a child. Not to fix them or change them, but to allow them to be with their pain, their fears and to be present with them so they know they are not alone and their experience, whatever it may be, does not have to define them, or shape their life's journey.

I learned that the psychosis I had experienced was those unexpressed parts of me; my anger, rage and pain. Once I acknowledged my emotions and felt them, they didn't have to control me; they no longer plagued my mind. When I had learned to see every experience as a gift, an opportunity to grow, to learn, everything changed.

Lauren Hornby - UK

I dedicate this chapter to my family, for their continuous love and support.

RESURGE EX CINERIBUS

The Art of Feminine Beauty

Surrender to Love

Surround yourself with all that's good;
Be the person you know you could
Kind and patient, caring and forgiving
Life is hard, but it's so worth living.
The lessons we face are all a test,
But don't give up, just do your best.
If we take a little and give a lot,
The world will feel the love we've got.
Share the joys that love can bring,
Smile and laugh,
Dance and sing.
See the world through the eyes of love,
From the Earth below
To the heavens above.

Annie Heggie - UK

Transformation #5

From Comfort Zone to Confidence Zone

"I refuse to give up on myself"

I have suffered from anxiety and depression since my early twenties. It still appears but not as crippling as in the past. If you've ever been anxious, you will know what it's like to freeze. You fear communication with others on every level. You go into hiding.

I often felt like a recluse and sometimes mildly still do. I've learned to deal with it so that I can function. I am learning to edge myself away from these barriers by helping other women push through theirs.

I've had many pivotal moments including post-natal Depression that lead me to quit my job. Subsequently, I felt the need to become more active inspiring me to become a personal trainer which encouraged me to take action over every single aspect of my business.

My main pivotal moment is quite recently due to my husbands reduced working hours at work. To make matters worse, he's on a zero hour's contract so we cannot be sure when he will work the hours needed to provide the wages necessary for our needs. It was at this point I decided it was me who had to become the breadwinner. I had been treating my business as a hobby. I love being active, so I created a job out of it. And why not?

At this point, I had no idea who I was training. All I knew I trained mainly women who could escape for an hour or two from their homes. My sessions were escapism not just for them but for me too. It was so difficult to keep the secret of my rough financial patch, intensified as my confidence was crippling me.

Now, those who know me, always see me happy and joyous as that is my usual face to the world. At work, no one needs to see my lack of confidence. I make myself comfortable in my work and my environment. It's my haven. As part of my purpose, I love seeing and making others smile.

At home, I didn't want the kids to see that we were struggling, but at the same time, we are very open and honest with them about what lack of money can do. They don't receive pocket money, and they know they need to work to earn it. Turning around this lack situation has made them all think of little business ideas to bring in extra pennies to spend.

Meanwhile, understandably my confidence was low, and I knew I had to push through a barrier and break out of this crippling but ever so safe comfort zone. I needed to know who I was teaching, the people who I wanted to help directly. I needed a good kick into action! I needed a business Personal Trainer!

I meditated to clear my mind and looked for clues, so I knew what I needed to do. I worked harder and put in more hours at the expense of my family and children. My business was nowhere where it needed to be. I believed I needed to work harder than ever.

I saw programs for 'lose weight in 7 days' 'lose weight quick'. I'm an observer. I observe what women do. We want everything fast, especially weight loss. We follow people who eat in a way some of us find impossible. The reason most women find it impossible is that they miss the foods they love. They feel restricted. Then when the weight loss slows, they move on to the next trainer, the next program or quit. Knowing this made me determined to adopt a different approach.

Then two things happen:

1. Someone came to me for advice saying they lacked confidence and needed to see me so they could 'get back out there.'
2. Someone shared a video with me about how exercise feels for longevity rather than weight loss.

Eureka I found my unique selling point! I decided to ask my long-term clients why they came to sessions. Everyone gave the same response; they loved the happiness and fun in the session but not only that they loved the confidence boost, better mood and lessened anxiety. They weren't interested in the weight loss, even though they all shed fat.

Do you know what too?

It is how I feel when I shed my weight. The weight loss was a side effect. I loved the feeling, and the fat loss became a bonus. Consequently, I was able to go beyond my comfort zone. I needed to! I started my eight weeks, 2 Step Transformational 1-1 personal training program. The results are guaranteed if it's followed! No one uses scales. We measure and photo. The results are evident. My diary filled. But I knew I couldn't be everywhere all at once because my family wouldn't see me. I've always wanted to go online and again I felt scared and paralysed! Filming videos are beyond me, and I prefer writing. However, I knew making videos was the step I needed to take so I can help others. Now, this took extra courage and more than two months to put my programme online. It took a while to complete because I wanted it to be perfect. During this time an article appeared regarding overthinking and no time is a perfect time. Nothing is perfect, even me. Things can be tweaked and changed like everything in life.

Take this chapter, I required the confidence to write it, and yes it has been mega scary. But I did it!

I now help women overcome the fear that exercise brings, build confidence along with lessening anxiety and depression. It's not a cure; I make that clear. I help women walk into an exercise class for the first time, attending a gym these are fears that we all experience. These steps have produced amazing fat loss results, although the fat loss wasn't the goal. These amazing women have the courage and confidence to step out of their confidence zone, from leaving the house to climbing Ben Nevis!!

Helping women see that it's actually 'how you feel' that brings amazing results. Consequently, I put my 'Active Ladies in the Spotlight' to inspire many others. But not only them, but it also keeps inspiring me to never give up on myself and my quest for confidence, lessened anxiety and not wanting my body to fall apart as I age.

What did I learn?

To overcome barriers, let go what others think and their opinions. What counts is that you overcome your obstacles so you can help others break through theirs; whether it's how our body looks, what we write, what pictures you take, to how your social media looks. We think of everyone judging our every move. Maybe they are, maybe they're not, but it's their opinion, and they are entitled to it. Don't let it stop you from going out into the world and living the life you want. Refuse to give up on yourself.

Trina Kavanagh - Nottingham, UK

I dedicate this chapter to my beautiful family

Transformation #6

Awakened and Walking in Wisdom

"I always wondered why somebody doesn't do something about that. Then I realised I am somebody."

Lily Tomlin

Ladies, Women, Goddesses, Girls – It is time for you to step out of the shadows. It is time for you to realise ALL your potentials. It is time to wander the path less travelled. The hour has come to hear and heed the call of the wild within and the calling of your true nature. The hour has come to take off your shoes and to feel your connection to this Mother Earth. Now is the moment to let go, to dream and imagine. Now is the moment to allow your Inner Child and Inner Goddess to rise. Now is the moment to begin the wondrous, revealing and exciting journey to connect with your super consciousness

My journey began when I was 26 years old with drug taking. I was suffering from low self-esteem because I felt I didn't fit into mainstream office jobs even though I was good at what I did, something was always missing. All of my friends were male because I felt I couldn't connect with women due to having a strong masculine side to my energy borne out of living in a rough area. At the time I was avoiding women because I was afraid of my femininity and power. It is a well-known fact that the right-hand side of the brain has an active link to our feminine power. It is creativity, sensuality and wonderment reside. At this point in my life, I was covering up the fact that I had a psychic ability because of the reactions and comments of others. I met a partner who re-ignited my calling to use this gift for the benefit of healing others.

When something you're so afraid of you to avoid constantly it has a way of creeping up on you and I ended up becoming an escort. Working in this way was the total opposite end of the pendulum, but it gave me a sense of understanding my feminine power. Further more I was able to understand the human psyche deeper because of the people I associated. There were a diverse range of individuals from gangsters to millionaires, poor men to married men and couples and ladies. Ironically this restored my faith in human nature as this essential basic human need of love, understanding and valuing individuality was I felt it was missing from my family and friends.

Whatever stage of life you feel you're at from the lowest point to the highest transformation you have within you the tools, understanding and passion for unlocking, feeling and re-igniting all you desire. If you ever feel you're worthless and drawn to drugs and life of self-abuse, then my suggestion would be to reflect on your routine of self-care, self-love and your environment. I would urge you to start writing things down like journaling; this can include pictures or even voice recording. One of the essential things you must consider is reaching out to those people you connect to who can facilitate the unlocking of your potential.

Walking side by side, we can achieve so much; sharing knowledge, experiences, thoughts, feelings, letting go of what no longer serves you. Replacing it with a new inner knowing, a glowing, with all your varied experiences, new ways of thinking and finding ways to allow feelings to work with you not against you. When you see what no longer serves you in a new light you can give thanks to ALL your experiences, find forgiveness; feel love and move forward with grace and ease. It is possible, and with the new energies transpiring this planet right now, we can become all we desire. The power is within you, within every single one of your 75 trillion cells. It runs through your DNA as it upgrades, re-informs and re-ignites within what you have always known; that you are a beacon of light and on a transcending journey. You do have a destination, and now it is time to choose just what version of you, you wish to experience. Time to dust off the soul, drop the masks and find the authentic, intrinsic nature of what it means to be a woman in an ever growing world of infinite, endless and multifaceted possibilities.

I am very fortunate to have reached a delicious place of inner self-knowing that isn't definite or stagnant, fixed or entirely formed. It is free from much misconceived self-formed and misshaped opinions; free from any projections of others wants, needs, ideas or judgements in my life so that I can become the Mistress of my Destiny. I am fully wide open in thought and nature while at this very time, even as I write this chapter, I am greatly reaching outside of my comfort zone and I can finally say I am beginning to enjoy doing so immensely. In this success, I connect with my Inner being so I can, along with the techniques, magical moments of revelation, and healing embrace what I never knew existed until now.

I'd like to share my Truth with you. Having experienced much self-loathing and self-harm, I urge you to awaken your awareness to your destructive behaviour and make changes. You may experience daily pain; mental, physical or emotional, do you need to endure this a moment longer? Perhaps you have been a victim of abuse or control; trying to or overcome addictions, do you feel sorry for yourself? Maybe you prefer to run away from trouble rather than face it, or blame others for your mistakes or attract volatile and rocky relationship is that the peace and solace you seek?

Find someone who can assist you to make the changes you need to expand and be the person you are meant to be. It's time to find a more spiritual path that will help you to find the inner calm and love you desire. Take a chance to meditate, find a form of exercise that you cherish rather than avoid, eat healthily every day, but don't forget the treats and seek the life you desire.

Willow Sterrick – High Wycombe, UK

I dedicate this chapter to my mum, Kathleen Sterrick who always challenged the status quo, free thinking, and pushed many of my boundaries as I did with her and in turn, we became better people for it and cleared up many misconceptions we had formed about one another.

The Art of Feminine Beauty

Mandala Hamsa

Orit Adiri

RESURGE EX CINERIBUS

Transformation #7

A Path to Power

*"Living with regrets destroys your Soul. Loving
your dreams will set you free."*

Growing up in Hungary, life was humble. It was quaint. My mother worked at home to take care of me, and our lives were simple. We watched my father go to work to drive a lorry every Sunday and stay away until the following Friday or Saturday. This routine was normal for us. Then, when he changed jobs, it would be weeks before we saw him. I missed him and yet I didn't.

My teenage years were like the youth of any other good girl who only longed for some connection to her father. I went to school. I came home and helped mum. I enjoyed going out with friends. It was normal not having him there. Even though he was rather stoic, he was bent on giving us the best he could, except affection. Don't get me wrong. I knew he loved us. But as a child, you know when something is missing because he never said words like, "I love you", yet he gave me life but never showed me he loved me for it. My father was stern to a fault.

Each Sunday morning, I'd wake up; prepare myself before I walked into the kitchen for breakfast. Dad and I would nod at each other in passing. No hugs. No kisses. No interaction. But I loved him anyway, to the point that I longed to hear from him how he felt about Mum and me.

After moving to the UK in 2005 and marrying a wonderful, wonderful man in 2012, I would take our son and return to Hungary to help my mum and my brother. It was so hard to see them suffer. Dad was holding his own. Despite it being emotionally draining, I would go and offer my support whenever I could.

On one particular trip, we found out my father had cancer. Sadness riddled me, but how he managed to handle it all was impressive; although he'd changed from that strong man to a harder, even more, distant man. I believe "I love you" was no longer even a thought in his mind.

At one point after he'd stopped driving, he had a notion that he'd like to take care of animals and arranged to do so. He loved his animals. Taking care of them, gave him something to look forward to when he was no longer driving. Sometimes I wondered why they made him happy, but I couldn't. On another one of our visits to Hungary at Christmas, we found out that he had sold the animals he'd grown to care and love so much. I could feel how this was affecting him. I could feel his sadness. He wasn't the same stoic man he once was. He's softer, gentler. But he still refused to say the words, "I love you." He just wasn't capable. But I understood his feelings.

The words that I'll never forget, where those he uttered to tell me that we would bury him in the spring. I stopped in my tracks, taken aback by this unusual statement. Who decides something like this? How do you come to know when you'll die? I soaked it up for a second and let it wash over me.

We went back to the UK after the holiday, and sure enough in the spring, I received the call that he had died. He knew exactly when his body would give out and cave into the disease that had ravished him.

This foretelling is one fact I couldn't shake. My father told me. He knew it. He DECIDED it. The power of the mind is phenomenal.

At that point, things changed for me. I began to understand just what we hold in the magnificence of what's in our skulls. I could never be the same girl I was before. Was my course to find my happiness? However, it eluded me for some time. I couldn't find my mojo anywhere. I knew that after being a working woman, staying home to take care of babies wouldn't satisfy my place in this world. That's when I hired a coach. I hungered desperately to know what I needed to do to make myself happy and to raise a happy, healthy family with me at the helm of our home. There's an entire population of the feminine that says I'm wrong. But my body tells me that being at the helm of a happy home IS my place. I could feel something deeper stirring my soul.

I had journaled while mourning my father's passing. But something was still unsettling; still missing. As I was journaling one day, something took over my hand. I'd been writing for a while when, all of a sudden, continuous ideas came to me, flooding my brain. I couldn't write fast enough. Pages and pages filled up, on their own. When I finished, my face and the table below me soaked with my tears. I had no idea what I'd written; except I'd written my future.

It was at that time when my struggle to find out who I was and what I am meant to do – my purpose – was over. My destiny is to be part of this world; to make sure that no one else dies without having lived their dreams. It's a message that I do not KNOW, but that I LIVE.

At that juncture, everything changed for me. I continued to be at the helm of a happy home. I found a way to live my calling, not just my children. My soul began to calm down and ramp up at the same time. Now that I knew my reason for being here on this planet, there was no way I could NOT make it happen. I entered this foreign world of coaching and everything I knew suddenly dissolved. I was in a place new and exciting, and the challenge of creating a brand new business from nothing with only my two hands has been the second best thing that's ever happened to me.

My first client validated every single emotion I experienced when journaling, ended up becoming my new life. She blossomed during the work we did together and developed a positive mindset to meet all the goals we set together. I knew then, I was on the right path. I haven't slowed down, and I continue to work with girls who know they have dreams but just have no idea how to make it happen with the power of their minds.

Now, I get up every morning knowing what I have to do to show girls just how to make their dreams happen and I go and do it. My clients learn and grow; they make their dreams come true. Consequently, their families are happier too. What I do in this world has such a profound impact on people that it is with the deepest gratitude that I wake up every morning to serve, not only my family but the families of the clients I coach.

Life is truly magical.

Anita Smith – Hungarian living in UK

I dedicate this chapter to all the girls who dream but are afraid to go after them. You cannot live this life with regrets.

RESURGE EX CINERIBUS

Transformation #8

Reality is Negotiable

'When I let go of what I am, I become what I might be'

Lao Tzu

Reality is confusing to me. When I'm talking about reality, it is the way things appear right now or the state of things as they exist, as opposed to an idealistic or notional idea of them (the dictionary definition of reality). A bit like Schrodinger's cat reality is not recognized until you see what forms from your thoughts.

Let me explain.

Some would say that I was born with a silver spoon in my mouth. My parents lived on Park Lane and 5th Avenue in New York City when I was brought home from the hospital in May 1966. My father, an ex-Jesuit seminarian (that's another story!) was a celebrated New York editor of his day and recognized as a first-class theologian with two degrees in metaphysics. Everything changed after Vatican II. Together with my mother, a gifted artist and writer herself, they created (through their company and together with colleagues) the entire Catholic catechism, reflecting the extraordinary changes from Vatican II for the United States Christian Brothers schools, then funded by the US Government. This project was well funded until President Nixon pulled the funding on Catholic education in US state schools in the 1970s. That was a difficult time for my parents and a temporary end to glory days. That's not to say I have a 'very poor to very rich' story; I don't. It's more like 'riches to rock and roll'. I never really wanted for anything and we always had enough, but there were plenty of financial difficulties.

Throughout my childhood, I attended eight different primary schools and three different secondary schools (and have two university qualifications). Without the internet, in those days we moved around a lot, so my mother and father could be in the right networks to attain work. My brother tells this amusing story. Whenever we moved to a new town, I would take him by the hand (me age of 7, him age of 4) and we would knock on doors one by one asking: 'Do you have any kids our age we could play with?'

At school in the USA, I learned that anything was possible and you could be anything you wanted to be. Most people wanted to go to the moon. I just wanted to look after the small animals that I felt were speaking to me!

But my journey through my childhood has been more about the people I met along the way. Always the 'new girl' at school, always saying goodbye to dear friends, I discovered a deeper way than culture, than social status, than skin colour to connect with those I could trust along the way. I learned to trust people based on what their energy is like (what I mean is how loving, how connected they are) rather than what they have done/who they are regarding culture, status etc. In my understanding, in my sixth sense, there is an environment, a palpable field around each person that lets me know if it is safe for me to be with them. That's how I describe what some people call a person's energy field, and it remains my most important beacon for connection and love: the way I relate best to people in all areas of my life.

My family mostly lived in the USA until I was twelve years old: we then went on holiday to Ireland with my family, and we stayed! I then went to secondary school and university in Dublin with a brief stint at the age of 12 at a boarding school in the West of Ireland (run by nuns). It was quite a culture shock, going from the USA to a boarding school in the West of Ireland, I can tell you! Sadly, at this school prejudice happened to me. As 'the American girl', I I was punished by the headmistress every day for arbitrary reasons. The usual format was that I was brought into the headmistresses' office and slapped on the hand with a ruler. Ten lashings were the norm. I could say I don't trust nuns now, but that would be unfair. In a sweet little cottage, about 500 yards from the imposing grey school building lived the retired sisters. Knowing what was happening to me, they would invite me in. Their kindness was overflowing. They sat me down at the turf fire where they would offer me a selection of the best of cakes from traditional Irish home cooking, and little, comforting tones of understanding. They were my beacon in a relentless, invisible storm. I lasted less than six months there, and left nearly fifty pounds in weight lighter, despite all the cakes. It took a while to work through those experiences in later life, I can tell you!

One of the most valuable lessons of my life is from my sister, a person whom I admire more than anyone in the world and who has achieved so much despite being severely disabled with cerebral palsy. What is most interesting about my sister is how she created 'can' from 'cannot'. She cannot walk. She cannot feed herself. She is not physically able to look after herself. The 'reality' is that she should not be able – at all- to do what she does.

The first paradox is that she lives on her own. She has a team of the most amazing personal assistants, all heart-warming individuals each who are the golden lights around her. She created her team; she motivates her team, her team looks after her, she looks after her team. Mary is one of the pioneers of the Independent Living movement in Ireland. She lives in her own home which is purpose built for her needs. Mary has a Master's Degree in Modern History from Trinity College Dublin. She finished her dissertation in one of the most challenging times of her life when she experienced three accidents all in the space of three months which now means that she has a pump for the delivery of morphine to ease the pain in her back.

Mary is a painter. She enjoys painting. Although she is hardly able to manage a paintbrush, she has had her paintings exhibited at the Princess Grace Library in Monaco.

And of course, there are lessons from my parents– who taught me to become responsible for myself very early on in life. Watching my three boys grow up has been my most recent joy – having children teaches you so much about yourself, the shortcomings, and the playfulness in life through a child's eyes. I wish for them only happiness – to find love in whatever they want to do in life. Allowing them to explore their childlike unbounded joy, I believe, is the greatest gift you can give to your children: the gift of their own best self.

People who know me in business call me a gentle but powerful person. I can understand people's intentions on a deeper level because of my early childhood experiences. Energy techniques are convenient in a business setting and are probably my secret superpower.

Nowadays I don't get stuck too often, and this is where reality gets confusing. I've reached a stage where I now understand how I don't let reality define me: how the seeming state of limitation of what we see before us is just that, a limitation: a fixed version of what might otherwise be mutable which depends on the lens from we view our reality.

I now see that it is also possible to be defined by our dreams, instead of by our reality. Therefore, it is right to me that anything is possible, and reality is negotiable.

Bonnie Harmon – A New Yorker living in the UK

I dedicate this chapter to the dearest people in the whole wide world to me: my mother Pat, my beloved sister Mary, my Brother Mark and my three boys Mark, Patrick, and Sean.

RESURGE EX CINERIBUS

The Art of Feminine Beauty

What is love?

Love is brown, Love is long
Love is blue, Love is you
Love is lean, Love can be mean
Love is strong, Love may be wrong
Love is bright, Love is light
Love is compassion, Love is in fashion
Love is wide, Love may hide
Love is sex, Love may perplex
Love hurts, love squirts
Love may shine, Love is mine
Love is in the heart, Love is in another part
Love is in the head, Love is hate instead
Love is lost, Love has a cost
Love differentiates, Love underestimates
Love matters, Love flatters
Love is deep, Love is to keep
Love lasts, Love broadcasts
Love is returned, Love is unearned
Love is kind, Love is in the mind
Love takes a leap, Love makes you sleep
Love is attention, Love is affection
Love is...........

Donna Wilkinson-Clarke

Transformation #9

When the Darkness Lifts

"It is during our darkest moments that we must focus to see the light."

Buddha

A story of how one girl, after many years of denying her voice and her truth, finally found the courage to say enough was enough.

I was trapped. Trapped in a life that I didn't want to be a part of anymore. I craved something different. I had spent so many years suppressing myself and what I wanted, always following someone else's ways or ideas. I did what made others happy. I had surrounded myself with people who I was now realizing did not have my best interests at heart – they seemed to drain me. For every positive step forward I tried to take, my boyfriend seemed to drag me back further. Our relationship was toxic, in my mind I was trying to help him, when in fact I recognised many years later that I was enabling him to continue on his path of self-destruction.

I was tired, scared, exhausted; both emotionally and physically. I had stopped taking care of myself and pretty much stopped caring about anything at all. I was depressed, on antidepressants, suffering with awful anxiety and severe IBS. I was a mess. I prioritised his needs over my own, time and time again; slowly but surely chipping away at any self-confidence or self-worth I had left. I tried many times to reach out of my darkness, to those who were supposed to love me and received nothing. My confidence was shattered, my self-esteem at an all-time low, I was lost and helpless.

How did it come to this? Is this really what my life is destined to be like? By this point I truly believed that I didn't deserve any better. That this man in my life, because he was good looking and charming, deserved to be placed on some sort of pedestal, and that I somehow owed him something for even being with someone like me. This went on for several years, progressively getting worse, and the situation darkened.

One day a moment of clarity hit me like a wave; if I continued to remain in my current relationship, with this person who I had given everything to, who I'd tried and failed to help many times over, with all the many issues he brought with him. I grasped that it was an impossible task for me and I couldn't fix him, in fact, I was just making him worse.

Ultimately, if I continued to stay with him, he was going to drag me into a world of unimaginable darkness, more so than I had experienced already, if that happened, it was unlikely I'd be able to make my way out so easily - if at all. Call it survival instinct if you want, all I knew is that enough was enough and if I didn't start to distance myself from him, he would take me down with him.

So what did I do? I got tough, I got stronger, I started to think of myself first, and something I don't think I had ever done before. I was twenty four and I wanted more for my life.

I started spending time on myself and with myself, I had always hated my own company and knew that deep down, this was part of why I continued to allow negative people into my world. I began to listen to my inner voice which was trying to guide me and tell me so much, yet I had silenced it for so long. Outwardly I seemed happy and confident, resilient to the situation I found myself in. I used to get compliments on how I looked, but I never believed them, it made me feel uncomfortable and awkward. I never truly believed people when they complimented me, always suspecting an ulterior motive, so accepting them was always difficult. However, once I started working on me and seeing for myself what others had seen in me for so long, everything began to change.

I have lived through the darkest of times. On the brink of losing everything, all because I allowed myself to be led and influenced by others, because I didn't have the strength to stand by my own thoughts and feelings. I didn't like myself, let alone love myself, but once my relationship with 'me' became more positive, my expectations including my relationships with others, increased massively. I am a great person to know, I make a great, caring and loyal friend and a fantastic partner. I believe that I am now someone worth knowing. It wasn't my high expectations that were the problem, but the people in my life not being good enough to reach the bar I'd set.

Fast forward many years and I am now thirty six years old, a mum twice over and married to the most amazing man. I started in network marketing towards the end of 2016, a big part of what I have learned from my first company, is that you need to work on yourself and any blocks that may be holding you back. In the happiness of a supportive partner, two pregnancies and a couple of house moves I had not been spending time on myself and for different reasons, had begun to lose myself again.

That prompted my decision to start in network marketing; I am definitely not a nine to five person. I believe there's more to life and I feel passionate about striving for more. The mindset work and motivation have helped me deal with what was left from the dark times I had experienced in my younger years. I am now confident in my own skin, self-assured and positive in my outlook and where I know my life is going. I have found an amazing product that has helped ease my IBS symptoms by 95%.

I want to help others find financial freedom, to look after themselves from the inside out. So many wonderful things can happen, when you truly take time for you and discover what makes you tick.

My Mission is to help and inspire women to make time for them; assist them in looking after their mind, body and spirit, empowering their discovery of how to 'Be true to you'. I want to encourage them increase awareness of their health and wellness, improve their self-belief and how they talk to themselves; how their energy flows and the importance of thinking and speaking good and positive thoughts. Learning the importance of what you put out, will always come back to you.

I know the thought of making yourself a priority can seem daunting, and to deal with the repercussions from others as you start to build yourself up, growing in strength and moving further away from them can be scary. But the truth is, those negative influences in your life will not like what you're trying to do and may well try to put you off and deter you, they'll try to make you doubt yourself, my advice to you is DON'T LISTEN!

Moving towards the 'true you' and a happier more fulfilled life. We are the creators of our own destiny, once we shift our mindset and start to step away from whatever or whoever is holding us back, absolutely anything is possible. Support during this time is so important, coming from someone who has lived in the darkness and been surrounded by negativity, lost and scared and fearful of change. I know you can do it. Amazing things happen when you really start working on you and your needs.

Step by step, take my hand and we can walk this path together. You are not alone.

Kate Young – Essex, UK

I dedicate this chapter to my wonderful Ray; a constant in my life for so long, seeing me at my worst and still loving me. I'm eternally grateful for all you do. I love you.

RESURGE EX CINERIBUS

Transformation #10

Enjoying the Food Twice

"I destroy my enemy when I make him my friend."

Abraham Lincoln

Never let anything, or anyone convince you there is only one way to achieve your goal. If it means you are restricted, living a lie or living someone else's life, then you must find your way.

Nearly in every school class, there is one kid that is overweight. You know the biggest one in the class. In my class it was me!

I fell in love with food ever since I can remember myself. I was considered to be a 'good eater' and repeatedly told I was a baby who loved every dish offered. I heard a comment about how I 'enjoy every bite' and friends of my mother asking her why does she not restrict my eating.

Although I was a very active child often playing out, climbing trees and even going to ballet classes; the energy used was nothing compared to what I consumed. Add to that my fondness for rice, pasta and potatoes and a dislike to vegetables then you get the perfect formula for weight gain.

It's not that the weight gain didn't bother me; it did; especially when I wanted to dress like my class mates with fashionable clothes.

Disappointingly, nothing fitted my size in the children's clothes shops, and I was still too short to fit into teenage or adult sizes.

I remember my mother taking me to another area of the city, well away from display windows. Inside were mainly adults and lots of clothes' railings. It was a shop for individual sizes on the 7th floor. My mother tried to convince me the clothes were just as appealing as the ones in the children's shop we visited. But they weren't. The material was awful, and I didn't like the pattern on it. It is no wonder I developed a dislike to shopping for clothes.

Being on the verge of adolescence, I decided to do something about my weight and the way I looked. Typically as a teenage girl, I was seeking the attention of a boy in my class, and I knew that the way things were I had no chance of attracting him. With the help of my mother, I was on a restricted diet of the food I disliked. Eating half a grapefruit for breakfast and being allowed only one slice of bread a day was hard to follow, however, due to my age, I was also starting to grow taller. Over a short period, I became what I thought was thin.

The truth is I was average for my age. Strangely it was at this time I also experienced my first ever migraine.

Back to my weight loss. Compliments were flying from many people including my mother's friends who had known me from childhood. However, one afternoon, outside of my primary school gates, the mother of the boy whose attention I was trying to attract said to me, "Well done. I thought you were hopeless and would grow to be a big woman." With these compliments a terrible fear surfaced. What if the magic disappeared and I go back to being the 'big girl?'

This thought began my unhealthy relationship with food. I was starving myself or living on a limited amount of fruit and vegetables only or consuming food I considered to be 'fattening' just to throw it all up straight after. The bulimic practice was the only way I knew of keeping my weight at bay.

The close people around me, like my mother and sisters, knew about it. I mostly denied what I was doing. It had become a family joke when I was leaving the dinner table and heading towards the toilets, that Orit is enjoying the food twice, both on the way in and out. The older I became, my situation intensified until at the age of sixteen my periods stopped for nine months. My body was simply not functioning as it should.

Emphatically I refused to be seen by a gynaecologist, so mother took me to a vegan Doctor who devised an eating plan for me. Two weeks later my period returned. I was back to normal but not quite.

Despite taking some action, my eating disorder remained - my secret friend. It was now a way of life, and I didn't know how to escape. Over time, I developed a scale addiction. I was obsessed. Without fail, I checked my weight every morning making sure the needle didn't shift to the right. I was living this way for forty years. It went on through two pregnancies and parenthood.

I was trying nearly every diet that came to the market. Some worked, some didn't, but none was sustainable as a lifestyle. Once I stopped following any diet, the weight piled back on again. I intended to reach my pre-pregnancy weight. I was obsessed with it and was never happy with the way I looked. All my friends told me it was impossible to lose the weight as the body was changing as we age.

It was after a winter break that I wanted to lose the weight I had gained. I decided to research on a diet that will be healthy and sustainable. I educated myself, took a course and taught myself about healthy ways of eating. I combined this with all the new knowledge from parts of diets I had experienced in the past that were under the criteria of 'healthy'.

In three weeks I lost all that I'd gained in that winter break. I 'liked' what I was doing, it was working fast, and I felt good. I decided to keep this system as a way of life to sustain the weight. To my surprise, the weight kept dropping, and soon I was back to my pre-pregnancy weight. Success!

Three months later I noticed the migraines, which had been part of my life ever since adolescence, were nearly gone. From three attacks a week I was down to once or twice a month, and remarkably they were not as severe.

Eight months later my scales broke. My initial reaction was of panic. What am I going to do? I had to buy a new one. But then in my head came another voice and asked, "Do you need it? You have been the same weight for the past eight months. You know what you are doing."

I decided to try living without the scale for one week. After that, I gave myself another week to see if there was any difference. Since that day, I have never bought a scale. Six months later I went to a friend's house and weighed myself. Miraculously, I was still the same weight. I could now release the secret that had burdened me for most of my life.

Being chained to diets or scales is a thing of the past. I am never hungry. I am healthier than I was thirty years ago. I have tons of much-needed energy being the mum of two boys, and now I am helping other women to return to their pre-pregnancy weight, gain confidence and love their body and life again. The greatest gift from this whole experience is I know that I can achieve anything I want in life, and you can too the pivotal moment you make that crucial decision.

Orit Adiri – Israeli living in Manchester, UK

I dedicate this chapter to all the women out there who struggle with their weight in one way or another. I inspire them to build a healthy relationship with food, to respect their bodies and to free their mind.

RESURGE EX CINERIBUS

The Art of Feminine Beauty

The Camino Way

The Camino way, is an 800 mile Spiritual Pilgrimage walked by St. James spreading Christianity through Europe ending in Santiago, Spain.

Pivotal Moments Co-Author Barbara Byrne completed the 100km journey to achieve her certificate for the Marie Keating Foundation, a cancer charity. She raised over 2000 euros for her efforts.

Barbara's strength, courage and grit are apparent as she intends to lead a group, 17th-24th April 2018. Stepping outside of her comfort zone is evidence of Barbara's Pivotal Moment Transformation.

RESURGE EX CINERIBUS

Transformation #11

Life's Disasters bear Great Gifts

"A women of substance has the courage to overcome tough times in her life and pursue her goals because she stands up for what she believes in and never gives up on her values and virtues"

"You do not do it for me anymore."

With these eight words, my husband ended our 22-year-old relationship, without further explanation and all I had lived for and believed myself to be; crumbled. To say this appeared out-of-the-blue is an understatement. Just three days earlier we had celebrated our 15th Wedding Anniversary at an expensive restaurant, leaving our two young sons in the care of a babysitter. I had carefully chosen a labradorite crystal in the shape of a star as my gift to him. My message "you are the star in my life". Cards with loving words exchanged, champagne dinner enjoyed and all in all we spent an idyllic hand-holding romantic evening that left me feeling blessed to be with the man of my dreams all these years on.

"You do not do it for me anymore."

From the moment he uttered these eight devastating words my life changed. "This cannot be!" I told myself, utterly bewildered and in shock. But I knew deep down, on hearing those spoken words, there was no going back. My heart completely was broken, a cliché I had previously heard but never understood - until that point. The end of my twenty two-year relationship started a harrowing chapter in my life in which pain; fear, devastation and insecurity became the norm. Seven weeks later he packed two bags and moved out into the waiting arms of a younger woman.

What I haven't told you is that we had transferred to the Philippines from Hong Kong just five months previously. And so I found myself stranded in the midst of my ship-wrecked life with no network of close friends and no family to support me.

At first, each day was a struggle. I didn't know who I was or what I was going to do. We had two young boys of seven and nine, and I had their needs to consider. I didn't want to take them away from their father as they were at such a vulnerable age and adored him. I needed to understand what was wrong with me? What had I done that made him toss me aside in such an uncaring, unfeeling way? What on earth was I going to do?

I had a very dysfunctional childhood and all the buried feelings of never being "good enough" which I thought I'd left behind me, rose up and engulfed me like a tsunami. The emotional and physical pain was like a red hot poker piercing my body. Had it not been for my boys, I don't know that I would have had the strength to carry on. And so began my challenge and my journey of self-recovery and discovery as I slowly regained the courage to be myself once more.

Over the next five years, I took small steps to rebuild my life, often three steps forward one step back. I built an incredible network of friends and became involved in the local community. I was a qualified Kinesiologist, Reflexologist and EFT practitioner, so I had these mind-balancing skills to help me, but I was compelled to delve deeper, not only to understand why this had happened but to work through and remove the negative and limiting beliefs that had seemingly taken permanent residence in my mind. I so desperately needed to understand and to discover who I was.

What emerged as I threw myself into my journey of self-exploration?

- Understanding that I had a choice; sink or swim, I chose to swim.
- Understanding that no one has the right to expect to be loved when you don't love yourself
- The importance of consistent practice of mind-balancing techniques and skills to bring myself back to a place of calm and the 'present moment' instead allowing my mind to control my thoughts
- The importance of taking one day at a time.

I came to realise that underlying all my insecurities, was a lack of self-love. Somewhere along the line, I had relinquished my power by always putting the needs of others before my own. If you love yourself unconditionally, there is no room for the feeling of fear, bitterness, and lack of self-worth or self-doubt to enter. And so I forged ahead, for the sake of my boys at first and finally for MY benefit, finding MY way one baby step at a time.

My pivotal moment of inner clarity and transformation is still clearly etched in my mind. One of my stress-relief strategies was to take myself on a long daily cycle which I stuck to, come rain or shine. One morning, flushed by the feeling of achievement after a particularly challenging ride the message "I'm done!" came into my mind. That was it! I was 'done'. Woohoo! I was ready to move on!

It took seven years, but I had finally regained my confidence and knew I was willing to go it alone. I made plans to return to the UK with my two boys to start a whole new chapter in our lives, with me now firmly at the helm and excited at the prospect of taking charge of my destiny. This decision was a massive challenge, and 'YES' it was tough, but I knew if I could do this I could do anything. So I began planning to find schools, somewhere to live and pack up our belongings after 11 years living overseas. Uprooting our lives proved that the hardest part of moving was leaving behind all the incredible friends I had made and whose support had been so crucial to me in my darkest hours.

But I did it, and I have never looked back. I believe that life's challenges always bring you a 'gift'. The gift I received from those eight words my husband delivered that seemed so devastating at the time helped to make me the strong, independent, compassionate woman I am today. I am proud of who I am. I am proud of what I have achieved. Above of all, I am proud of how I have brought up my amazing sons and who they have grown up to be.

I can never thank my ex-husband enough.

Fiona Clark

I dedicate this to the wonderful friends, (you know who you are) who took me out of the dark into the light on so many occasions. I thank you from the bottom of my heart. I also dedicate this to women who feel challenged by some aspect of their life.

RESURGE EX CINERIBUS

Transformation #12

Fear, Friendship and Faith

"When I trust the inner knowing, I surrender to the guiding force that leads me to the right direction"

Fragrant Heart

2016 was a year of discovery! My relatively "comfortable" life disrupted as I discovered my fears, faith, forgiveness, friends, deepest feelings, courage, creative talents and love.

It started out as an easy year; things were moving along routinely and smoothly until I sensed a change in one of the closest people around me. It wasn't tangible; I just knew that things were different and that my life felt like it was about to be changed significantly.

Without warning or explanation, the upheaval started, many quarrels occurred in my marriage. Torn, I knew that I could not continue along this path. I also knew that the time had come to say 'goodbye' to this chapter in my life, but I was afraid. I was scared of the unknown, what if I failed? How will I provide for my daughter? What would my life be? What would people say?

These doubts continued for many months creating anxiety, bouts of depression and many sleepless nights until one day; my daughter hurt. There was a disagreement with her dad, and this single episode became a very nasty encounter. It felt like someone had dug a deep hole in my heart, the pain was unbearable. Will it ever get better? My life seemed so hard with all the animosity! Life was unfair! I hated him with every cell in my body! How could I hurt him? Where would I turn?

I kept thinking about how life changes in such unpredictable ways. These thoughts consumed me every waking moment. I felt as if I would burst, the thoughts wouldn't leave me. So one day I sat at my desk and started to document all the thoughts that were running through my mind. These gave birth to my first poem. It took me about three days to record and edit. I felt relieved. The pain has dissipated and it no longer felt unbearable. The creation of this poem was my catharsis! I now felt ready to conquer this battle!

Things and events didn't continue smoothly, but they improved. By this time, I had no more doubts and knew what decision I had to make; it was time to end the pain, the suffering and move forward with courage and strength. But how would I do this? What's my next step? Do I travel this path alone?

Trusted friendships help us navigate our way through the mire. My daughter received an invite to one of her school friend's birthday event. While the girls swarmed and played, the three of us (mothers) spent the day lounging by the pool drinking rum punch. We talked about everything, and eventually, the topic of relationships arose. Sharing my marriage was over revealed we had a lot more in common than our daughters. We were all going through changes in our marital relationships. We bonded, and the pre-destination of our meeting meant we could help each other. We have cried together, laughed together, and helped each other in the rearing of our children. Our friendships made my journey easier. I no longer felt alone; encouraged there was now only one direction, and that was to keep moving forward.

During the period of uncertainty, I learnt to trust my intuition and believe in myself. I knew that it was time to further my education and I also felt that I couldn't even attempt it at this tumultuous time in my life, but every obstacle that came in the way of registering for the MSc Marketing course, removed with little effort. The ease of which was a sign I was on the right path. I didn't know how or why I just knew that I had to pursue these studies.

Classes started in September, and my husband announced his relocation to another country. I felt like he had deserted my daughter and me. How would I survive classes at the university? How would I juggle my daughter's transport to and from school? How would I be able to help her with homework when I had my own? Many negative thoughts flowed; I didn't have the answers only a strong belief it would work out. The readily available support of friends and family was one valuable lesson for me that taught me the strength of my faith. Without having the answers, my needs met as I embraced trust in God as I moved forward. My power of faith was one of the most defining moments for me.

Pursuing these studies also diverted my attention in a positive direction. I had a burning desire to learn all that I could on the subjects in my course. Concentrating on my studies meant that I no longer focused on the hatred, the pain or the hurt. Instead, I practised many meditations for forgiveness, self-love and enjoyed the time my daughter and I spent together. My heart felt like it would burst with joy and on the happiness chart it was increasing. Energy goes where the thoughts flow!

Even though I am still on this journey, I am confident that everything happens for a reason and a season. I feel blessed to have discovered my creative talents, I've written over twenty poems in the last year. I am convinced that my experience was designed to enhance my teaching skills, discover my talents and assist me on my path of self-discovery. My life will never be the same; it will be better!

Alison Watson - Barbados

This story is dedicated to my daughter Alystra. She is wise beyond her years, full of good counsel and very inspiring. She brings me joy and light. My darling may you experience the joy of self-discovery.

RESURGE EX CINERIBUS

The Art of Feminine Beauty

Perfection

There comes a time
When actually, fine
Just doesn't cut it anymore.

And in that cogent,
That pivotal moment
Just what the hell is it all for?

Deception.
Perception.
Perfection?
Sarah Rossellini

Confidence Flower by Trina Kavanagh

RESURGE EX CINERIBUS

Transformation #13

Call of the Soul

"The cave you fear to enter lays the gold you seek."

Jung

When was the last time you heard the call of your Soul; faced your Dreams and pondered whether to give up that vision or dare to take a chance to make it your reality?

We begin in April 2016; I was living in London and working in a School in Chiswick, splitting my time as a Teaching Assistant and running the Outdoor Education program. My life was fast; I cycled to work fast, did my job fast and I even tried to relax fast. It doesn't work. This fast paced lifestyle was having a significant impact on my health and nothing the NHS was offering helped, so I took a chance on an acupuncturist.

My pivotal moment came a few weeks after a session with her where she said, "Samara, there is nothing more I can do for you. Your body is asking you to change your lifestyle. If you carry on as you are, you are drastically shortening your life." Maybe that isn't the words you want to hear from your Alternative Therapist, but I was unlikely to get this reality check from a conventional Doctor, and my acupuncturist gave me the kick I needed.

It was around this time I was applying for my GTP place, Graduate Teaching Training, at the school I was working. All my colleagues were sure I would make a fantastic teacher and would walk the interview and lesson demonstration. In fact, they were so certain it was hard not to believe this was the right path for me. The Friday of the Lesson observation arrived, now I can't remember what we were exactly learning, something mathematical, not my strong point by any means, but I was applying for a primary GTP, so it was a good foundation lesson to show. Once the lesson was over, I stepped into the Interview process with the Headmistress from one of the Sister schools in the Syndicate.

Her name was Joan, and she was an incredible lady, South African, soft yet authoritative. I remember the interview so well; I said everything I needed to say to show her that I was the candidate of choice. It was like something else was speaking through me, and even I was a bit shocked at the eloquence of my words. I remember a distinct moment where Joan asked me about what I felt the purpose of education was; my heart opened as I spoke about how for me, Education needed to allow children to discover their Authenticity and let that shine out. The trouble was there was a small, yet very loud part of me screaming, "You don't want this GTP place!"

The interview ended, and I left the room feeling flat, even offering the place to me was certain, and I also knew that the small, loud voice was right. I didn't want this opportunity. My colleagues were so excited for me and insisted on going to the pub to celebrate as it was the last Friday before the end of the term. I didn't feel up to it, so made an excuse and cycled home.

That weekend I sunk into a black pit of despair. I took myself out for several fast paced walks along the River and through Bushy park and shut the curtains on my top floor flat. I distinctly remember one of the mornings crying and praying to the Universe that I would not be accepted into the GTP program, begging for any excuse to avoid my Soul's voice and the life changing decision it was asking me to make.

Monday arrived but saved from the confirmation email, which arrived late on Tuesday afternoon. Knowing being offered the GTP place made my whole body sink. There was no running from it now. I remember I ran down to see my friend and Line Manager, Emily, and tell her what was going on. I was pacing up and down trying to find the right words, "Em, I got it, but I don't want it!"

Her face was a picture, she sat me down and told me to stay calm and to think about it, but I knew I didn't want the offer. In fact, the relief I felt was enormous; it was like the whole room suddenly filled with light. The next day I cycled into work with determination, it was the day before the end of the Easter term. After the morning assembly, I went to the Headmasters office and said, "Gordon, I can't accept the place on the GTP training, and I am also handing in my notice." I cried at this point, more I think with relief but also with a deep sadness, teaching was an old story and not my destiny in this life.

Thursday morning was the last day of term, and once again I stepped into Gordon's office and handed him my letter of resignation. He looked at me, but what I met was a sincere kindness and acceptance. He told me, "Samara, you are brave, go and follow those dreams that call you, go build your place in the Forest."

We sat for a long time and chatted. As I left the Head teacher's office I knew I had made the right decision, even though I had no idea where I was going or what I was to do next, I knew I had said Yes to my soul, and opened up a huge space in my life for that possibility to come in.

My journey since that day has not been easy; I left behind a career, a pension, a life and the safety net of the Known to walk head long into the Unknown. It takes courage to walk the Pathless Path, but as a Shaman and energy healer, that is the Path I walk, and I love it, even when the passage is hard, and I am staring down the barrels of a gun held by my own Shadow.

My life is not about having the best car, the best house or drinking champagne, in fact, it is the opposite. I long for simplicity, watching the sun rise, feeling the rain kiss my skin as she falls from pregnant clouds; I long for a Life less ordinary, where I can stand up and Be all of me and in so doing, allow others to be All of themselves too and above all be Real.

In my understanding, this is how the World changes because when we do this, we come to own and accept all of ourselves, which is incredibly powerful as well as challenging. Every day I wake up and thank my Soul for calling out to me at that moment, giving me back my choice, so I could say 'Yes' to it with all my heart and walk this Extraordinary life.

Samara Jacobs – Reading, England

I dedicate this chapter to all those that have been before and all those who will come after, the Earth Keepers and Altar Keepers, who work with the magic of the very Earth so that when we lose our way, this Voice sings back the song of our Souls.

Transformation #14

Passing the Test

"Where thought goes, energy flows"

Tony Robbins

For me, there was no dark hour as such. I was already in the dark; I just didn't realise it at the time.

I was twenty one and was working as a beauty therapist in deepest Oxfordshire. For those of you who are familiar with or live in the English countryside, towns are often miles apart, and buses are a thing of legend and mystery. I lived seven miles away from work and other than relying on my parents' goodwill for a lift every day; I knew I had to pass my driving test.

However, I had already tried and failed my test three times and this latest morning had seen failure number four. Sad and dejected I sighed my way into work. My friend Gill worked in the therapy room two floors below me asked me how it had gone. Gutted, I told her.

'Ah, come with me a minute', she said smiling and lead me into her room.

I had spent two years at Beauty College and two years working in the big wide world as a beauty therapist, and in all honesty, I thought I knew everything about the human body. I knew all about the bones and the tissues, the origin and insertion of the muscles, I could label a 26-point cross section diagram of the skin, almost with my eyes shut. So when Gill told me she was going to talk to my body, I was a tad curious.

'Let me do some Kinesiology with you, Kinesiology is the study of muscle movement, so first I'll need to muscle test you', she said.

'Muscle testing is a way of finding out how your subconscious mind thinks and feels about something'. Gill explained.

'Hold your arm out and resist my pressure when I try to press it down'. Easy, I thought and resisted I did.

'Now think of your driving test', she said, and to my amazement and surprise my arm dropped. I had no resistance to her pressure whatsoever!

Like a scene from a bad horror film, my head turned sharply towards her. 'What did you just do?'

'Nothing', she replied calmly, 'You did that. That's just how your subconscious mind feels when you think about your test.'

I was completely stunned! How could this be possible? How could I seemingly lose control of my body? Worse than that, my mind had gone blank, and I felt like everything I had ever learnt was suddenly erased. In that one moment, a blinding flash of realisation hit me. I knew nothing at all about the human body; there was something much, much bigger going on inside of me. It had nothing to do with the outside at all; it was all about what went on the inside.

After allowing me a moment or two to recover myself, Gill showed me a simple but very effective Brain Gym® technique to use myself called 'Positive Points'. This practice helps to remove any emotional stress from your mind. I held the palm of my hand very lightly on my forehead and thought through all the aspects of my driving test for a minute or two until my mind began to wander. It was that simple.

Gill then asked me again to think of my driving test while she redid the muscle test.

This time I was able to resist, amazing! My body stayed 'switched on', and my arm muscle remained steady. I also felt calm and clear in my head, and I no longer had that awful panicky feeling in my stomach.

Next time I took my test I remember staying calm even when another car pulled out in front of me, which before would have made me freeze up and fail. This time I stayed focused and went on to pass my test. I was so pleased with how easy it had been.

Your subconscious mind is much like a six-year-old; it always wants to be happy. Positive thoughts flow more easily around the brain and body than negative ones. A negative thought seems to change the internal chemistry somehow and cause 'roadblocks' along those neural pathways.

Brain and body are one system working together so when a stressful thought appears your body responds to it. This stressful thought will 'switch' you off for the briefest of moments and slightly weaken your muscle strength. The good news is a positive thought will 'switch' you back on again, and if it doesn't, uncomplicated body based movements and exercises such as Brain Gym® can help. My life path had just taken a massive turn. I no longer wanted to run my Beauty salon. I wanted to go back to school! I just knew I had to learn more about these incredible body based techniques. Learn more about the mind and body connection; about Kinesiology and muscle testing and certainly more about how one very easy, almost too simple exercise had managed to clear my mind numbing panic in minutes.

I went on to qualify as a Brain Gym® Instructor, a Neurological Kinesiologist, an Energy Therapist, and much more besides.

Bodies fascinate me. Brains amaze me. How we think and feel, affects us every single minute of the day and how quickly we can help heal ourselves just by holding points, making precise movements and practising specific techniques.

As human beings, we are an incredibly beautifully, brilliantly designed, hugely complex yet amazingly simple organisms. We are so much more than skin and bone. It is all about what goes on the inside.

Next time you find yourself 'switched' off or panicking about something, I encourage you to give the Positive Points exercise above a go. It's the automatic hand on forehead movement we all naturally do when stressed. This time just focus on the problem a little longer until your mind wanders and your body calms down. The solutions truly are all in the palm of your hand.

Carey Boyce - She

This chapter is dedicated to my amazing teachers –
Gillian Hindshaw and the unforgettable Katie Blyth.

RESURGE EX CINERIBUS

The Art of Feminine Beauty

Feel the Flow by Carey Boyce

RESURGE EX CINERIBUS

Transformation #15

An Act of Self-Acceptance

*"Loving ourselves through the process of owning
our story is the bravest thing we'll ever do."*

Brene Brown

This is the story of overcoming a decades-long struggle with self-acceptance and love.

There was a time when I dealt with my chronic physical pain and mental illness with copious amounts of alcohol, and sometimes a pharmaceutical (and at the weekends a recreational) drug — or two. I used these as a crutch to "get out of my head", but at the time never considered it to be a problem. This was mainly due to the fact that I was lucky enough never to experience hangovers until the age of 45. During the week, because I had to get up the next morning for work, I would have an entire bottle of wine or a six-pack of beer to myself to wind down from the day. And that was before any social drinking occurred, which would no doubt end up in a binge to see who amongst my friends could drink the most.

Although I didn't consider the amount I drank a problem (others I knew drank much more than me and were still functioning — at the time), it didn't take a genius to see that my health was suffering as a result. But seeing as chronic illness runs in my family — metabolic syndrome, type 2 diabetes, rheumatoid arthritis, pernicious anemia, Epstein-Barr virus, you name it and someone has got it — I grew up believing that being sick, fat and tired was just normal fact of life to those who were unfortunate enough to be genetically predisposed to such conditions, like me. In fact, good health was something that was never discussed in our house because nobody was ever in good health.

The ironic thing was that my father was an architect who specialised in building hospitals. Yet still, someone in my family was always sick. The big illnesses were dad's type 2 diabetes and mum's rheumatoid arthritis. On top of that they were both obese, long before it became fashionable. As a small child I remember being embarrassed about my mother walking me (very slowly) to school, because I could see how the other mothers and teachers looked at her. I remember one of my classmates asking me "Why is your mother so fat?"

Then I started getting sick. From the age of 7, I was also going to doctor and hospital appointments, because that's what we did. And then I started getting fat and fatter and sicker. For many years I was so depressed that I wanted to die and the physical pain endured during six years of chronic fatigue in my twenties added to that.

So by the time that cold, dark and damp late November morning came around, I was an obese and toxic mess. Standing at my father's graveside, I only felt numb. "I should be freezing," I thought, because it was beginning to drizzle on top of the biting cold wind that was coming in from the coast. I was only wearing a lightweight black PVC jacket on top of my black mini-dress and turquoise-coloured tights... always the rebel. But I didn't feel the cold. I didn't feel anything.

That meant the valium and red wine that I had swallowed after breakfast was kicking in. And it was working a treat, because at this point in my life I didn't know if I could handle any more pain. Physical or mental, it didn't matter. I had had enough pain already. This numbness, this was the exact feeling I was after. I was slightly taken aback by the bugler playing *Taps*. My dad had served in the US army as a young man and apparently this was a thing. Being a pacifist, this ceremony was not what I was expecting. "This isn't what it's like in the movies," I thought. But no one else seemed to be questioning what was happening, so I just stood there. Numb.

As the soldiers folded the flag and then presented it to my mother, I shuddered because I knew this was it. Dad really wasn't coming back, even though the man I had seen a day earlier lying in the coffin didn't even resemble the man I once knew. And that image in itself was something that took me ages to get over — I couldn't sleep for months because every time I closed my eyes, I saw that shell of a human that was supposed to have been my father. My mother held the flag in her arms as my dad's coffin was lowered into his grave. This really was it. "I should be crying like the others," I thought. "No, it's fine because you have to be strong for mum and Greg (my brother)," I also thought. But I didn't know what to do because all I felt was numb.

And then I heard it: "GET HEALTHY!"

"What?" I asked to myself? And I heard it again, loud and clear: "GET HEALTHY!" Like a flash of lightning my ego chimed in: "Was that me? Who is that? Am I talking to myself? WHAT? Healthy? Are you kidding me? How the hell am I supposed to do that?" However, I KNEW in my gut that if I didn't listen to the call, that I would be following my father into my own grave sooner rather than later.

That cold, dark and damp November day was 10 years ago and that moment literally changed my life. I now know that when I heard "Get

Healthy", it was the voice of my higher self gently letting me know that that was what I HAD to do. So get healthy, I did. I began after a chance encounter with an amazing homeopath, who put me on the road to detoxing and eating clean. After releasing 40lbs in the space of three months and feeling better about myself, I began my reflexology training, something it had taken me five years to do. Through the understanding that in order to heal others I had to be healed myself, I joined a gym and began getting strong for the first time in my life.

Throughout these 10 years I've done many things, including studying energy work and metaphysics, writing books and becoming a certified personal trainer, mainly to prove to myself that I could do it.

I shall honour my father's passing this year by being the happiest and healthiest I've ever been in my life — at 53. I want you to know that it's never too late to change your life. Your body is ALWAYS telling you what it wants from you.

You just need to become consciously aware and listen.

Theresa Fowler – London, UK

I dedicate this chapter to Gi for believing in me.

Transformation #16

A New Year - A New Beginning

"You cannot connect the dots looking forward;
the dots can only be connected looking backward."

Steve Jobs

She heard the yell from upstairs; her eldest child shouted and had been pushed by the male adult at the top of a steep stairwell. The man followed him down the stairs, the baby in his arms; menacingly yelling, screaming then turning around and punching the wall. That was the moment she knew she had to go that was the point that she had to finish it.

It, whatever it was, had been going on far too long, there had been too many lies, too many mind games and her limit reached.

It was New Year's Eve; she knew there was no point in trying to leave again right now. She knew it would be more hassle than it was worth, so she settled her eldest and came back downstairs again to face the music.

Her husband told her, he wanted a word; only to tell her she's at fault. She should be supportive of him. In a calm and assertive voice, she said, "Enough is enough; no more"; she wanted to enjoy the evening. He wouldn't have any of it. He kept on and on at her. Again she told him, "Enough is enough." She wanted to go for a walk to give her husband time to calm down. He wouldn't allow her; he kept shoving her back to the bed, taking her boots away and blocking the door making it impossible for her to leave. He continued to badger her; he was relentless. Finally, the baby started crying, but she knew he would not let her go and comfort the child. She knew he would insist on going himself.

His lack of presence gave her a moment, so she grabbed her boots, and her coat, tiptoed into the attic bedroom to snuggle with her eldest. Her racing mind provided a plan; to run away in the morning.

She received texts from him, contrite and apologetic as always, wanting a pleasant evening. But she was wise to it now, and she knew that nothing ever changed, in fact, she decided it was time to establish a new standard, as things increasingly grew worse. She realised like the frog in the boiling pan of water if she didn't jump soon, her strength would lessen.

Her emotions were running high as she put her eldest in the car. For his sake and safety, she knew she was doing the right thing as she drove to her mother's house. She drew her breath as she sipped on a cup of tea. She knew she couldn't go back for her youngest alone; she knew that he wouldn't hand him over. She called her brothers for help, they wouldn't help they told her to go back and make it up and if she needed to leave to do it at another time. Too much had happened and she couldn't go back not now or ever again. She wasn't going to stand by and watch things get worse day by day.

On the advice of a solicitor friend, she contacted the police. She knew it was her best chance of getting him to hand over her baby. Of course, he acted surprised as the police appeared at the house with her. Despite her husband's behaviour, she was unable to remove the child from his care without involving social services. The police stayed while she collected some belongings and also reassured that she would see her baby later.

She was unprepared for what happened next. In the blink of an eye, her husband dropped the 'Mr Nice Guy' act, beginning by withdrawing all financial support despite knowing she was still on maternity leave. He restricted access to the house too, making it difficult for her to retrieve her belongings. Solicitors letters soon dropped through the letterbox with his requirements and constant threats of court but most of all she was unprepared for the lack of love and support from her family, treating her as if **she'd** done something wrong.

Everything is temporary, and this too would pass. She was sure of it; it was a case of hanging on in there. Better things would be on the way; she knew it. As the saying suggests, "Sometimes the situation gets worse before it gets better." Even her work had become a battle. She wasn't sure she had the strength for it; so she drew her strength from her two boys. There were nights when handling her situation was a struggle; she had no support, and surrendered to her fate.

On these nights her eldest would wake her up and tell her he could see a man at the end of the bed. She'd say it was his guardian angel checking on him; then he would say a prayer and snuggle down to sleep. It was uncanny even in her darkest moments she felt protected and that everything would be ok.

Her battle continued as her husband showed no signs of leaving the marital home, suffocated by this unbearable life, she arranged for a storage firm to take away all the furniture, he had only contributed a chest of drawers and a coffee machine anyway. The rooms were somewhat bare after she had put all her other essential items in the car. She had resigned herself to a living space at her mother's that felt cramped and claustrophobic, but it would be temporary.

He finally moved out. She was able to return to the house so the children could feel settled. However, he continued to play mind games with his demands. He threatens court but can't afford it; he wants a reconciliation, but only on terms, and the stress of having children from previous relationships is too hard to bear. She understands from her actions that she has made the right decision as he would never be a real stepfather and her son deserves a better life; so does she.

She felt incredibly grateful for trusting her instincts to write and document everything; this was important now. She knew that the court would be able to see through all of his lies and that the truth is always more powerful.

The judge found everything she said to be true, and the court ordered him to have supervised access once a week. He chose not to take it. She was finally free to live life on her terms.

Natalie Bird – Manchester, UK

I dedicate this chapter to my sons; to all those who supported me; and to all women who feel trapped and afraid to trust their instincts that better things are on the other side of the darkness.

RESURGE EX CINERIBUS

The Art of Feminine Beauty

Woman

Alison Fennell

RESURGE EX CINERIBUS

Transformation #17

Life – A Bumpy Ride!

"Never say never, because limits, like fears
Are just an illusion."

Michael Jordan

Being completely honest I have never wanted to say there was something wrong with me. I only told a selected few, but Brenda Dempsey mentioned about her Pivotal Moments book idea, and something struck a chord, and here I am telling my story.

It all began back in the early 1990s; I was approaching my 40s.

My children were growing up, and I had gone back to work part time. It was a good life, but I'd started getting regular headaches some migraines too. One day was so bad I was wobbly, had double vision, something that had never happened before, so I booked a doctor's appointment.

I saw a lovely young lady doctor who put me through a series of tests and then said I should go to the hospital straight away. She gave me an envelope, but I said I couldn't go straight away as I had my girls to sort out and a lift to the hospital. She said, "Just get there ASAP."

A little later I arrive at the hospital, where I waited what seemed like for ages; maybe an hour. I am then seen and admitted; glad I went home for a wash bag! My head is getting worse, not better. I was seen by the consultant early evening. He told me I would have an MRI head scan the next day. The night went by and morning came. I had the scan mid-morning, and the consultant came late afternoon just to say that the scan was ok and I could probably go home next day and that was that.

Years went by. There were headaches, there was tiredness, then one morning I woke and the left side of my head from top to throat felt like I'd had a dental injection and it was beginning to wear off. I was scared. I phoned for an emergency appointment at the doctor's practice. I went along, given antibiotics and signed off work. However, it didn't improve. Luckily I had private medical insurance through my work, so I returned to the doctors and asked for a referral to see a specialist. Two days later I saw Dr.B a young doctor, he went through all my medical history and said he would get a copy of my earlier scan and I was to have another.

A few days after the second scan, I returned to the hospital. It was the worst day of my life. I entered the doctor's room, Mr. B said you've probably looked it up. I hadn't. The next words made my head spin. "I can tell you that you have Multiple Sclerosis (MS)." He explained. I was stunned, I said nothing. He continued talking about MS how different stages go and the only useful thing he said that day was when you get any illness or infection it will take double the time to get better. That was the only thing I took away from that meeting, and he said to contact him for another appointment if I wanted to at any time. At that moment I never wanted to see him again but thinking back now, he was a young doctor who could do nothing for me, and I believe he didn't like that, so he was just very abrupt. I left his office went home and cried and cried and wondered why life was becoming so hard for me.

The same day I told my family. They were anxious for me. I would not accept anything was wrong, so I changed nothing and later regretted it. I grew more tired with ease, and walking took its toll on my energy; it took me a while to realise I had to work this out. My family has been wonderful over the years always there for me, reminding me to rest and noticing when I do too much. They would try to stop me which was not that easy in the early days.

Over the next two years, I carried out lots of research, asked questions and spoke to my new doctor. She said that she would refer me back to Dr B; I didn't want to see him again I told her, so she wrote a letter but didn't get a reply, however, I received an appointment!

At first, I didn't want to go to the appointment, but I did. I pushed myself. Wow, what a changed man hhe was, so bright with me. He gave me confidence as he told me I was doing well and I only had to see him once a year. Now fifteen, years on we still just catch up once a year!

Today, I feel so good and blessed that it's not worsened. I have learnt to take notice of my body, and only once in a while, I have an episode. My family and friends are brilliant.

However, life can be a struggle, but it doesn't last. I always survive. Most recently I fell down three stairs and broke my ankle. Do you know what? That's life! When you embrace your mistakes and accept them for what they are you free yourself from guilt, anger and misery.

One last important thing. I believe in spirits and angels. I didn't believe at the beginning of my journey, but now I do. I have read much about archangels and know that Michael, Raphael and others are there for me bringing me comfort, guidance, and reassurance. I feel and talk to spirits, and I'm not mad!

"You have to believe we are magic. Nothing can stand in our way. You have to believe you are magic. Don't let your aim ever stray. If all your hopes survive, destiny will arrive."

- From the song 'Magic' by Olivia Newton John - written by Coe, Mollinson and Friederike

And finally just found this quote which rings true - My Secret's out.

"We are only as sick as our secrets. These secrets make it impossible for us to be our authentic selves. But when you make peace with yourself, the world will mirror back that same level of peace. When you're in harmony with yourself, you'll be in harmony with everyone else." - Debbie Ford

Annie Heggie – Woking, UK

I dedicate this chapter to my family and friends who have been there for me – you know who you are.

Transformation #18

Vulnerability

Let the shadows fall and fade away,

Slowly slip from around my hard shell,

Crumple into ripples at my feet

And leave me naked in front of your eyes.

There you look me in the eye

And you see me as I am.

Skin shining bright and imperfect

Body just held exactly as it is.
I feel my skin tingle under this gaze

Not of judgement but of curious grace.

I no longer look to hide,

What I once felt as shame,

But stand out and let the Silence form.

The pause between the breath; Mine and yours

Holds us in this intimate pose.

This is me, I am this

Made Vulnerable, buy not weakened by my choice

And in this state, only now can I see,

This new journey unfolding at my feet. *Samara Jacobs*

Transformation #19

Going with My Gut

"Be still and know that you are God."

For the last two years, I had felt that my life had "gone dead". Feelings associated with opportunities running out, of doors closing and a sense of sadness and hollowness about my daily activities that once brought me at least happiness and usually a joy, gone.

I am sure that the cause of it was menopausal as I was 49 when I sensed a chronic lack of interest and despair seeping into my life. But apart from hormonal changes I knew that something deeper was fueling these feelings. I often felt that there was no point in living and was taking antidepressants for a while.

Being a great believer in alternative and holistic therapies for some time, I have found that homoeopathy has helped my general well-being enormously since I first began receiving treatment from my homoeopath four years ago.

Being diagnosed with fibroids caused heavy and long periods. Further investigations also found an ovarian cyst. There was no sign of cancer though, and so I refused a full hysterectomy. My homoeopath had told me that if issues are not resolved at the point of their manifestation and only cut away, then they would manifest somewhere else in the body. These words resonated with me, and so I took the remedy and a month later an ultrasound scan showed the cyst (which my surgeon told me would need surgery) had gone.

With the continuation of the homoeopathic medication, my life improved. I had manageable periods, increased energy (I was no longer napping for an hour or two every afternoon) and my life expanded. Workwise I was able to run a weekly art class and do more exercise.

But the last two years had become unbearably sad and joyless, and although I tried everything I could to energise myself, I was failing.

A few months ago I became aware of Shamanism and dowsing via conversations and synchronistic events. A friend suggested we met at an art centre for a coffee. In the foyer, I saw their notice-board plastered with layers of posters, flyers and cards but one flyer drew me – it was for Cardiff Dowsers, and immediately I felt that I wanted to get involved, and I took the details down.

So – fast forward to the first meeting I attended – at the meeting was a craniosacral therapist. I felt a connection with her (she was not actually "billed" for that day, but the original speaker was ill and couldn't come) and decided there and then that I wanted a treatment from her. It was very powerful with my arm starting to "flutter" with releasing energy even before her hands touched me. I sensed pins and needles and sudden pain in the wound site of an old major surgery. Next came deep yawning – so much that I thought my jaw would crack. After that, a profound sense of bliss and calm washed over me leading to tears.

She told me that she had done shamanic work years before and this piqued my interest. That evening I contacted a local shaman and arranged an introductory meeting. Although I sensed she was a lovely person I did not feel a connection and so did not pursue it further. I did, however, find out more about Soul Retrieval following that meeting as I was receiving an extreme sense that this is what was at the root of my joylessness and lack of life purpose and direction.

Shortly afterwards, a lifelong friend suggested I contact a shaman who had carried out work on him years before. I found a video of her on YouTube and immediately liked her manner and voice.

On her website, I learned more about Soul Retrieval work and booked a session there and then but it was while I was reading more information on her website that I clicked on the words "Munay Ki" which informed me about sacred healing. What moved me was the idea that we are surrounded by and are part of a Luminous Energy Field which could be enhanced and used to connect with higher, cosmic energies as practised by the Inca people of the High Andes. Following my distant Soul Retrieval by telephone, I felt a shift in my perceptions about who I was and what had been missing in my heart, and I knew I would have to go on an upcoming Munay Ki Initiation Rites course with this particular Shaman.

The week's course was pivotal in that it gave me a new blueprint for living. I had never been amongst such wise and loving people before. I felt a lifetime of negative actions and thoughts being exposed and unshackled as we exchanged the rites. I was enlightened and grateful for this new awareness which I knew would increase with time. I realised that fear is at the root of all negative thoughts and that my biggest lessons were to give people and myself a chance and to avoid judgement.

Through sharing healing and deeply intuitive conversations with others I learned more about acceptance, trust and humility and I already see that the nature of my interactions with family and friends is altering subtly for the better. I am so grateful for this enlightenment.

I understand that everyone needs their story to be told and heard and that by allowing spaciousness and listening to come in, it will be possible. By enabling the being of others, I allow myself.

Going forward I am also more compassionate with myself so that I can give it to others as after the course I realised that everyone is just doing the best they can in this life and I do not have the right to judge or change anybody. The understanding of this revelation has completely taken me off the hook with regards to getting irritated with people or resenting their actions as I see that they have their path and I have mine, and each is equally valid and valuable.

The Munay Ki has shown me the sacred nature of all life and that I need to respect that.

Alison Fennell- Merthyr Tidfil, Wales

I dedicate this chapter to my mother and father.

Transformation #20

Fate Creates a Better Life

*"What sometimes breaks the physical body reinvents
the Spirit in the most amazing ways."*

Zeleen Teter

On 21 June 1995, I died in a car accident.

I was driving my new car I had received as a gift for my high-school graduation. I was only 16 years old, graduated high school in 3 years with almost a year of college completed and a full academic scholarship to the University of AK Anchorage. In other words, I was an uber-achiever

I picked up my two soccer buddies to go hiking at a near mountain pass called 'Hatcher's Pass'. Solstice is highly celebrated in Alaska, as it is the longest day of the year and the sun does not set. Driving down the mountain, we stopped briefly to use the outhouses. After that, we got back in the car. It is the last thing I remember.

I have a frontal lobe and posterior brain damage consequently, I have no recollection of what happened except for the near death experience.

Before I share the experience, note we had a dreadful single-vehicle car accident. According to the individuals in the car, I possibly fell asleep at the wheel. There are no shoulders on these Alaskan roads. I apparently drifted to the edge of the road, woke up, and overcorrected the car. The car flipped end over end and landed with my head going through the windshield into a tree. When the first Emergency Medical Team arrived at the scene, they covered me up so that no one saw my shattered skull - they obviously had great difficulty finding vital readings. At some point, a medical professional brought me back to life. However, no one seems to know when or what the details were.

I had sustained between a level 3 and level 4 LaForte fracture - I shattered every bone in my face to dust (except my chin). My parents had to provide a photograph so the surgeons could reconstruct my face. Over 100 titanium plates, screws, and mesh were used to put my face back together, as well as cranial bone grafts, cartilage grafts, and much more. I was hamburger meat.

When I was in the hospital, I first tried to remember what happened that fateful night. Frustration grew as all I could remember was our last bathroom break about 15 minutes before the car accident. There was one memory that I did not understand, but it was so profound that the more I thought about it, the more obsessed I became with it.

As I said, I don't remember the crash - just darkness. It was not a malevolent darkness. I was a sixteen year old adolescent who was not descending into any pit. And I did not feel any evil.

Being blinded during the accident is a possible explanation for having no recollection. The medics told my parents that I would be blind for the rest of my life, and to make arrangements - yet, somehow I can still see. I think my blindness, possibly, did not allow me to see "the tunnel of light" or to look upon my dying self. I have always felt alone in my Near Death Experience (NDE), as every other individual with an NDE story I know about; has seen a tunnel, hovered over themselves, met dead relatives, cliché, etc. My experience was wildly different.

I have never written down my NDE, and I have only described it to thirteen people in my life. First, I feel as if there are no words in our limited vocabulary to describe what I experienced. Second, whenever I describe my experience, weird coincidences happen. When I tell this story, something unexplainable happens to me or the individuals who hear it.

The darkness enveloped me. I felt as if I was transcending time and space. Imagine what it would feel like to spiral through the galaxy as an entity not bound by any gravitational pull or directional trajectory. That is what the experience felt like as I journeyed through the darkness.

What I know to be true is that the direction I was heading had no bearing - it seemed to be everywhere. It was like rain. I was like rain.

If drops of rain were souls and Heaven was the giant puddle that catches and pools all souls, then I was a drop of rain water that was following my path toward the puddle. I knew I belonged to the puddle. It seems like a strange analogy, but I cannot think of a better way of describing it. Like a magnet, this collective was drawing me in. There was no human emotion attached to it. I did not fear. I did not doubt. I did not question.

The only human emotion I could feel was pure, unrelenting, unconditional love. Take the unconditional love a mother has for a child and amplify it a thousand fold, then multiply exponentially. The result of your equation would be as a grain of sand is to all the beaches in the world. So, too, is the comparison between the loves we experience on earth to what I felt during my experience. This love is so strong, that words like "love" make the description seem lessened.

It was the most powerful and compelling feeling. But, it was so much more. I felt the presence of Angels. I felt the presence of joyous souls, and they described to me a hundred lifetimes worth of knowledge about our divinity. Simultaneously to the deliverance of this knowledge, I knew I was in the presence of God. I never wanted to leave. Never.

The next realisation was the sound of voices here and there. The noises of the Intensive Care Unit, nurses, doctors, people crying when they came near me. My eyes sewn shut, mouth wired shut, breathing through my neck, hair shaved off, face crushed.

My horrendous tragic accident happened years ago, and I have not found anyone else with my injuries who have survived. I rose from the ashes, like a Phoenix. I rose above to become more than a shell of the person I could have become. Or someone I was "supposed to be". Rather, I became the newer, better version of myself. I went on to obtain Bachelor degrees in Political Science and Philosophy, as well as other accolades without ever telling anyone I had brain damage. Despite everything that has happened to me, I am more whole now since I was crushed and broken. I had to build myself back up.
I am still building myself back up as I battle the physical consequences of that fateful night. I would never take it back. I am a beautiful Divine Spark. If I was not meant to be here for a purpose, I would not be here now. I have also found my gift. I am an empath with other abilities. I am now beginning to learn how to use these talents. The Divine does not take without giving back.

Zeleen Teter – Washington, USA

I dedicate this chapter to Ron W. Roush, the love of my life whom I found at the lowest point in my life.

RESURGE EX CINERIBUS

The Art of Feminine Beauty

Moving Meditation by Fiona Clark

Cycling is my moving meditation. It is the time I feel free, have a clear mind and the time I receive much of my inspiration and reach inspiring challenges.

The more I challenge myself on my bike the more I see the comparison to 'life'.

Everything we want is on the other side of fear and procrastination; hills that I used to dread and avoid I take now on with gusto!

I am about to do a 90 mile ride for the Princes trust from Buckingham Palace to Windsor Castle! 35 miles more than I have ever cycled!

RESURGE EX CINERIBUS

Transformation #21

You be you, I'll be me and together, let's be us

"We're all just walking each other home."

Ramdass

I remember it vividly.

Sat outside on a beautiful evening looking up at the stars, I heard that voice that came from deep within;

"You're meant to be with him. Go home" It said, as clear and as dazzling as the sky that night.

I had been pondering what was next for me. And now I knew.

What was that feeling? I wondered. Oh! It took me by surprise. That'll be love.

A couple of months later, we entangled in an embrace.
He looked me straight in the eye, deep into my soul, and said,
"You're holding back."
Taken aback, I thought, "How could he know?"
"I can tell" he continued as if he had read my mind. "I want to know all of you."

The guard of protection I had previously put up to protect my tender heart, had been there for so long; even I couldn't feel it. But he could. There and then I vowed to let him know the whole of me, no matter how scary it felt.

"You don't know what you have let yourself in for," I thought.

Seven years later, he held me again as I sobbed in the dead of night. I was anxious, afraid and my light had nearly diminished. I'd been on an autopilot of career building, people pleasing and style flexing and had lost myself.

"I've got you" he whispered. He felt like the lighthouse on solid ground, keeping me safe in the stormy seas I found myself in.

He asked me to write a list of all the things I loved; anything that lit me up.

"All that matters now is you and that you do more of the things on that list."

Within a year or two, life was unrecognisable. People remarked on how luminous I was and how my enthusiasm for living life, love led, inspired them to do the same.

I discovered ancient parts of me, long forgotten or drowned out. My healing hands that brought comfort to tender hearts; intuition and oneness with my soul that whispered knowing into my ears and brought visions to my minds' eye. I found a deep connection to life and nature in all its colourful and insightful wonder and an adventurous spirit that saw me soaring through life; relishing new and magical opportunities.

I felt it before he said it,

"I don't know that I love the person you are becoming." Thud! I was brought back down to Earth.

"You're not the person I married. I don't believe in all this stuff, the same as you. I want the old you back" he continued.

My heart was heavy for him. I knew there was no going back. Was he scared? I wondered. He wouldn't say.
We both tried to ignore the gap that was growing between us, but soon it was impossible to ignore. More change was on the cards.

The anxious feeling that I was losing myself returned. I felt I didn't belong in the corporate mold I had tried to fit into for so long. That voice deep within told me to follow my heart in its search for meaning and use my gifts in service of others who wanted to listen to the calling of their heart and be lit up by life. I decided to leap. He begged me to reconsider. So afraid my light would go out if I stayed and so certain I was being guided, I leapt anyway.

In doing so, I hurt his heart. He was furious I didn't care how he felt. I resented he didn't trust me. Our anger was masking a deep sadness. Like an ancient grief in both of us, it revealed the common connection that had been broken.

Despite his anger pushing me away, I tried to cling on as best I could. I invested so much of my energy into trying to prove my love to him, trying but failing to be what he wanted. I tried to talk, to explain who I was. But he didn't have the capacity to hear it. I could feel the guard around his heart, and it made me feel sadder than ever before. So did the fact I was leaving so many parts of me hidden when I came home. The parts that made me feel like a Goddess. The parts I most longed for him to see and experience for himself.

Months passed. I was exhausted.

"Tell me I don't have to lose everything; especially him! Surely, I'm not meant to let go of him too?"

I sat on the bathroom floor, shouting in frustration and anger, hot tears streaming down my face, as I clenched my fists and shook my arms in despair. Surely this couldn't be part of the plan for me. Our love, I remember seeing written in the stars.

"Just show me the way!" I demanded, the anger beginning to dissipate from my voice. I let out a few quiet sobs. My hands fell to rest on my lap; my shoulders dropped my voice no louder than a whisper now, "Please. I can't take any more of this. I'm begging you. Just show me the way."
I surrendered, and I was shown through the power of sisterhood to show myself mercy.

"I can't do this anymore. I've been trying, but you keep pushing my love away. I'm exhausted" I said. "I love you, but I can't love you at the expense of not being me."
"I know," he said and held me in his arms. "I'm sorry. How about you be you, I'll be me and together let's be us".

It took two years. We had to learn to unveil ourselves and rediscover the thread of gold between our hearts. We forgave. We taught ourselves to hold each other accountable to love. We ventured together into the deep sadness we'd tried to hide.

I learnt how to love myself enough to bring the whole of me even when it felt scary; even when my soul mate didn't understand. He surprised and delighted me in the ways he continued to show me the real depths of his understanding.

Deep down had he understood all along?

Returning from Provence where under another starry night, I reclaimed the very Essence of me, I brought my ancient Goddess home. He received her with open arms.

That night, in the flicker of candlelight, he asked if I would lay my healing hands on him. I could feel the cross he'd had to bear in inviting me to step up and rise. And with all of the gentle power of my heart, I lifted it away and laid it to rest.

Bethany Rivett-Carnac – High Wycombe, UK

This tale of love unconditional is dedicated, of course to my darling Johnny. Thank you for always guiding me home; for encouraging me to be the woman I came here to be. I love you, and I'll always and forever love what we've got. And for all those magnificent Earth Angels who held us in their hearts and supported us as we navigated through our stormy seas, thank you. You know who you are. We couldn't have done it without you.

RESURGE EX CINERIBUS

Transformation #22

Becoming Elizabeth

"Be authentically YOU and live life as who you are meant to be"

Sometimes self-harm leaves no physical scars. It provides no pleasure, pain, or punishment. It gives no relief and delivers no discernible feelings. Sometimes self-harm is simply too smart for us, creeping up in stealth-mode. It is cunning, secretive – invisible. Then one day – maybe, something happens, perhaps something usually inconsequential but it is enough. The world has shifted ever so slightly, the mask has slipped, and the dirty face of the trespasser revealed.

My story has none of the usual themes of darkness and light, the rise from despair, addiction, poverty or abuse. There is no triumph over evil or the glory of success against all the odds. Indeed I had a relatively normal (if there is any such thing!), middle-class childhood and a grammar school education. I had food in my belly and new clothes on my back, there were parties, holidays, birthdays with cake – my parents remained married until death did them part.

I have one incredibly talented beautiful son who makes me proud every day, and I can also claim a 25-year, international, corporate career, two degrees and plenty of other qualifications and experiences. I consider myself privileged to have climbed Mt Kilimanjaro to stand on the roof of Africa and to follow the path of Hillary and Tenzing if only as far as the base of Everest. There has been only one marriage but several heartbreaks. I have had money, and I have been broke - not so long ago there was a point where being homeless was too close for comfort. It's fair to say that there have been some pivotal moments in my life.

Strangely enough, it was none of the big ones that created the shift. I was always the strong one – resilient having the ability to keep going – even when my personal or professional world completely rocked. It was much later after most of the life-changing events had been consigned to history when I realised what had been going on for most of my life. As I looked in the mirror one day, I simply realised that I could not see ME! The person I thought I had become invisible.

Who I saw in the mirror was an old woman, a shadow staring back at me – a dull, lifeless, grey shadow that was no more than a ghostly image of what I once was. The face I saw reflected the measure of my life – the hurts grooved out in every wrinkle that marched across the pale skin, stark; rooted and meticulously formed, as the pain that caused them. Where was that carefree child with unlimited dreams? Where was the idealistic young woman, the girl who would change lives and change the world? Where had she gone? How had she allowed the life sucked out of her? Why had she given in to other people's demands, gone along with what they wanted, not spoken up for herself? When had she started simply be like the others? When did she lose her voice? When had she hidden her authentic self?

Saddened by what I saw I continued to look until slowly, almost imperceptibly a flicker of something forced me to look in the mirror, beyond the glass and to my core. Anger rose, and I pushed this 'THING' to the surface; bursting from the sorrow of my tears and with grim determination faced it for the first time. Staring that sad reflection down, I vowed that I would discover my true self again and become fully visible as the authentic me – the person I was meant to be.

I realised that the slow, creeping suppression of what made me unique was, in fact, a whole new and unexplored dimension of self-harm. It would be all too easy to apportion blame on the players that appear in my life story, but I recognise now that I always had the power to choose – I just didn't know it at the time. It was me that allowed the erosion of my individuality as I attempted to fit in. It was me who didn't stay true to myself – tarnishing my integrity as I agreed to do things I didn't want to. Only I can take the blame for not following my intuition and consequently not doing what I was meant to do and as a result lost my impact and influence. I was the one that was hiding in plain sight; I just wish I had realised it sooner!

A good friend of mine often says; "It is not what happens to you but the way you deal with what happens that makes the difference to what you achieve." I embarked on a healing and spiritual journey embracing Angelic Reiki, Rahanni and Munay Ki. Through increased spirituality and awareness I was gifted with a unique programme that helped me to make sense of what had happened to me and that I now share with others. I blend healing and coaching to help people rediscover their true self and enable them to live as 'who they are meant to be', allowing that authenticity to become fully visible – often as a first time in their lives. We are all different, and I recognise that like many things, invisibility with all its facets, can be measured on a spectrum. Where anyone is on that scale is subjective, however, as I continue my journey, the signs are more apparent. It is also clear that many people cannot see that they are hiding from the world. The scars, after all, are on the inside. They too are invisible.

Elizabeth Carney – Hampshire, UK

My story is dedicated to all the characters that played their part in it. Dead or alive - the good, the bad and the ugly, I have learned from all of them and their lessons brought me home to exactly who I am meant to be. I am Elizabeth - finally free to be Totally Me.

RESURGE EX CINERIBUS

The Art of Feminine Beauty

Self-Rising

Elizabeth Carney

RESURGE EX CINERIBUS

Transformation #23

Awakened Courage

"Every next level of your life will demand a different you."

Leonardo Dicaprio

The realisation of my pivotal moment is from a succession of whispers that became silent screams, the sighs before the cries and the pushes that became the final shove.

When I look back, it was not just one thing that leads me to my point of no return. It was an explosion of a hundred tiny little things. I thought I knew myself. I figured I was happy with my job, with my relationships, I thought I knew where I was going until suddenly I woke up. I stopped wanting the life that I was leading.

I experienced a rude awakening, as I realised that the person buried inside could no longer tolerate the person on the outside, and this façade had to go. My head could no longer organise my racing thoughts. My brain could not tell the difference between rational thought and an irrational one. Perhaps, I had taught myself to reason with an unreasonable world for so long that I had exhausted my mind with lies and bitter tolerance.

There was an emergency in my life, and that emergency was me. I was 25, single, working in a soul destroying job; monotonous retail, that was unfulfilling and scarcely rewarding. I had planted myself in an endlessly trying and thankless comfort zone, with nobody to blame but myself. Let me reiterate that, I was stuck in a comfort zone, during the prime of my life, and deep down, there was no comfort in it. It was an ignored, festered pain. Each month is adding to the precious years that I should have enjoyed my life, doing the things I loved, full of zest for life and I sat back and let my life happen to me because I felt that I was not worth more. I had no faith in myself, and I didn't believe that I had a say in creating the life that I desired. I needed a new challenge more aligned with me.

In those dark days, I felt that a happy life was a selfish life, something that you should not dare ask. So I buried my heavy head in the sand, and accepted my ill fate, with a forced smile, for as long as I could. However, as the saying goes, the truth can only be hidden for so long, and it's true. From what I have experienced, the human spirit, when given a glimpse of hope for a new life has an incredibly powerful and ferocious fighting spirit. I finally decided to take responsibility for my life. I felt unfamiliar in my flesh as I felt parts of me leaving and other parts clinging to me that no longer served any purpose in my life. My soul needed a doctor, and the only person who was qualified to prescribe me the right medicine, was, in fact, me. Nobody knows you better than you know yourself, all you have to do is have the courage to listen and take action. It was time for me to grow.

So that's what I did, I finally took responsibility for my own life. I quit my job. I sold my car. I booked a one-way flight to Paris to do a two-month fashion internship. I fell in love with the city straight away, so much that I ended up moving there. I am now in Paris, almost a year and a half. This city made me fall in love with life all over again. It was here that I shed my old skins and became a new me, the real authentic me. It was here that I finally decided what I wanted in my life.

The fashion Internship was a fantastic and once in a lifetime experience, but it also proved to me and confirmed in my heart and mind, that this contrived industry was not the one in which I wanted to be involved. I soon began to fill my days with reading, studying and learning as I found work with an English speaking babysitting agency just opposite the 'Palais Decouverte'. I studied French and childcare every morning, and after that I would work with French children in their homes, teaching them English in a happy, fun natural way. The children helped me connect with the inner child in myself and my outlook on life positively influenced by them.

I finally accepted and reclaimed my love for writing and devoted my time to poetry, scribbles and blog posts for websites that receive millions of readers every month. I started writing a novel about my soul journey and adventures in Paris, the remarkable people that I have met along the way, the ups and downs, and the beauty of life and the power of positive thinking. I have also qualified as a life coach and a re-write your life story coach. These courses lead me to my love for psychology, counselling and inspiring people to live the life of their dreams. I decided to further my education, and study a BSc Psychology with Counselling Degree online, while I still live and work in Paris.

I have learned that it's okay to do things in your own time. You have full permission to outgrow yourself. You are under no obligation to remain who you are if you are not growing personally, intellectually or spiritually. It is a sign, which you need to push yourself out of your comfort zone. You have unlimited potential; your personality, your talents, and skills have no cap. Introspection is essential if you want to understand yourself better. I have learned that I am not obliged to accept and believe every thought that I have, but rather observe and examine, consciously, why and what I am thinking. Every day, we are all influenced and manipulated, by people, media and society, that we can become moulded into a different version of our higher truth and calling.

We are programmed to forget our minds. The process of listening to your intuition and following the guidelines of your inner dialogue is simple, but not always pleasant, and that's okay too. I have accepted that, allowing yourself to become a new person, warrants great leaps of faith. It is imperative to have confidence in yourself. To stretch yourself, you must change your experiences and environment first. It is our experiences that develop our belief system. Life lessons are how we learn, expand and gain wisdom, through action and participation.

Every day, we have choices. We have an opportunity to remain stagnant and accept our fate, or we can actively, move forward and reach our own desired destiny. Now, I know, that happiness is not selfish, it's a birth right, and you must make a commitment to love yourself enough, to have the courage and build your philosophies, theories and beliefs that support you and the life you wish to follow. That may mean, leaving people behind, quitting a job or moving to another country. Maybe it just a factor, quitting that awful addiction you have. You know the answer already, you just haven't accepted it. At this moment, I feel so lucky and grateful that I went from being a person who needed help, to being the only person who helped me, and now the person who can help others. Breakdowns can only become breakthroughs, with the right attitude, persistence and mindset.

Life is a beautiful journey; the earth is a beautiful place. We only have one chance to make a beautiful story. Do not let one person or one tiny set back, or perhaps ten setbacks snap the pen from the hand that writes your life story.

Emma Stuart – Donegal, Ireland

This chapter is dedicated to my wonderful parents, who always support my decisions, are there to help me and offer advice, support and free hugs when I need them. I love you.

RESURGE EX CINERIBUS

Transformation #24

Acceptance

"If you do what you've always done,
You will get what you've always gotten."

Tony Robbins

As a child of the 1970s, I grew up in a world that was not so big or wide. My small cul-de-sac had around twenty houses, and my life only bounced between the street and my primary school, which was 15 minutes' walk away. Telly was just three channels, and we did not have a phone at home; the red phone box at the bottom of the road was the '2p' Mecca for communication. Everyone in the street knew everyone and everything about everyone. Kids played hide and seek until it went dark, or circled endlessly around the pavement on their bikes (I never did get a Chopper). Everyone's family had work - they were working class – down the pit, on the pot bank, for the council, in the steel-works, in the mill or had a trade. Everyone was in the Trade Union, and they all voted Labour. My step-dad was a lorry driver, and my Mum was a cleaner. Only one or two families had a car – people were not that wealthy – because the buses ran from early morning to take people to their labours.

On Saturday nights, families walked to the local Working Men's Club for a night out, to watch a live band and have a dance – but only till 11 pm closing time! Sometimes, we would go to the 'club' on Sunday lunchtime; adults to enjoy the bingo and the kids to visit the sweet-shop on the corner, for a paper bag of loose sweets from big jars on never ending shelves.

We did not have much, but we had enough. We had Sunday roast even if it was 'crisp' sandwiches on Friday for school lunch. We lived in a council house like all the other families in the street. Somehow new school uniforms and Christmas presents were paid for each year. As kids, we did not understand the relevance of the Friday night 'knocker' – aka the door-to-door moneylender – but he did a long round where we lived.

High school was twenty-five minutes' walk away, zigzagging through the local streets – I was ever thankful for the 9.30am start! I enjoyed school because I enjoyed learning and was quite good at it.

I was a Prefect and regularly saw the queue outside the Deputy Head's door, across the corridor from the Common Room. Muffled voices, then quiet, then the door flung open, and another kid walked spritely along the hallway, his eyes 'watering' and with his throbbing hands firmly pushed into his pockets from the caning. Corporal punishment was far more civilised than some of the openly aggressive behaviours in junior school – teachers dragging girls from the classroom by their ponytails for the slightest infraction and flying blackboard rubbers hitting their mark regularly with scary and painful accuracy for a mistimed prank. Not paying attention would elicit a clip round the head or an extended lecture from the teacher on behaviour that took you well past the bell. Some kids dreaded getting into any trouble at school because that would result in double the drubbing at home – the belt was a favourite method in some families. Then again, many of the mothers in these families had an uncanny habit of walking into doors, late on Saturday nights after their husbands got back from the pub, resulting in a black eye.

I was one of those kids who cried on her very last day of school. The big wide world seemed scary, even though it was not big or wide – probably only a couple of miles all the way around. It was 1984 and Thatcherism was getting well into its stride – the big, wide world was heading for a radical change.

Being working class was no longer something to be proud. Being raised in a council house was something to be ashamed. If you didn't own your home, you were some failure. Not having enough was somewhere between a crime and a farce. Unionism was a nasty smell that gradually eroded to almost nothing. Voting Labour just labelled you 'chav'.

But I was young, and I could work, so I embraced big shoulder pads and consumerism. I worked in an office (because I managed to do reasonably well in my O Level examinations) and I bought my first house when I was twenty years old – and sold it again nine months later when interest rates hit 18%. I drove my Fiat Uno – that I had a personal loan for - and went on holiday to Portugal (paid for on the credit card) and tried to forget those I left behind – in the street. Like many, I aspired to be middle-class; that was where it was at, after all. I almost convinced myself that I was, every time I visited the family, in the street.

In the decades since then, I have, in fact, met many people – working class, middle class and upper class - lived and worked abroad and returned home to visit the same street in which I grew up. It remains a real snapshot of the world we live in right now.

Today, I call myself working class because that is what I am. I no longer own my home, but I do not see that as a failure – actually, I have so much freedom as a result. The media still suggest that I should be ashamed of my council house upbringing, but I am no longer. I am proud to vote Labour and stand alongside others for more compassion for the people living in the real world. I am the person that my upbringing shaped. I have seen real life but have been lucky enough not to see the very worst of it. My experiences are something for which I shall always be thankful. I have been out in the big, wide world and have come a long way – to accepting myself for who I am.

Sarah Rossellini – Staffordshire, UK

I dedicate this chapter to S, you know who you are.

The Art of Feminine Beauty

Queen of the Ocean by Emma Stuart

A midsummers dream ended, eyes from blue to jade
I searched in the dark of the night to look for you.
Wet eyelids and a blurry vision; a faded shadow
You were nowhere to be found.
I surrendered my soul to the sky,
Followed the reflection of the moon
And I collapsed into the ocean.
As I looked up from below, I saw the other side of you.
I reached out, but I couldn't touch you
Now, all that the ocean resembles is shattered pieces of broken light.
Now, I swim in an ocean of sin, but
I do it with grace and glory
I rest my head on the bottom of the seabed.
I am the Queen of the Ocean; I live in no man's land
The shores shelter me; the saltwater cleanses me
I spend my days beachcombing the sands; Barefoot
Searching for inspiration, may find a piece of heaven?
All I find are brittle bones and debris of battles lost at sea
Buckets of broken dreams and abandoned ships
Swept away by the force of nature
But I refuse to be shipwrecked, so I just wait
And watch the changing tides
Hoping that a raging heart will find me
For it was love that brought me here
And it is love that will bring me home.

Transformation #25

A Journey to Teheran, a Personal Story in a Historical Context

Kibbutz Sde Boker, April 1977

At midday, I walk from the kibbutz school where I teach, to the communal dining hall, to join my family and the other kibbutz members for lunch. On my way, I pass by the rows of members' mailboxes to pick up our mail. My heart skips a beat when I espy an envelope addressed to me from the Israel Ministry of Education. My hands tremble as I tear open the envelope and scan the letter that informs me I've been offered a two-year contract as the principal of the Israeli School in Teheran, Iran.

The newspaper ad for this position caught my eye a few weeks ago. It offered possibilities for change and new challenges for which I was yearning. So I immediately wrote to apply for the job. In doing so, I was ignoring the fact that, on the kibbutz, the general assemblies of kibbutz members make decisions about members' employment-not the individuals themselves. Now there is an option for my family and me to embark on a new direction. Do we dare undertake it? I feel dazed and unsteady and look for a place to sit down and compose myself, so my agitation won't arouse the curiosity of others in the dining hall. Until Ya'akov and I make our decision, this thrilling news will remain our secret.

For several weeks, I struggle to maintain a calm exterior while a whirlwind of doubts fills my mind. Do we dare leave behind our home, our work and our friends on the kibbutz? What about the children? Tammy and Dror, in kindergarten and elementary school, can they come with us, but Yuval will have to stay at the kibbutz school to complete his final year of high school. How will he manage? What if the kibbutz won't grant us a leave of absence to work in Teheran? Will the rewards from the new challenge be worth the potential risks? The race of thoughts is dizzying, and sometimes I feel almost paralyzed. Then, at last, the whirlwind subsides, and we decide to go to Teheran.

Ya'akov and I drive to Tel Aviv to meet with a Foreign Ministry representative to tell him our decision. He describes Teheran as an exotic and exciting city, "so safe that your children will be able to play freely in the streets."

Israel's relationship with the 1 Shah Pahlavi's regime in Iran is now in its heydey. The two countries collaborate on matters of security, oil, business, construction, engineering, agriculture and more.

Hundreds of Israeli families live and work in Teheran, and their children attend the school where I will be the principal. Ya'akov and I return to the kibbutz and submit our request for a leave of absence to work in Teheran. Now our secret is out. Soon, the kibbutz general assembly votes to reject our application. In the months preceding our departure, our friends begin to walk past us on the kibbutz paths without speaking and avoid sitting next to us in the communal dining hall. In August, when Ya'akov, I and our two children board the plane to Teheran, we know that the point of no return. to the kibbutz has been crossed.

Teheran, August 1977

In the Teheran airport, my family and I stand together, overwhelmed by the crowd, the noise, the heat, the unintelligible language. Suddenly, a broadly smiling man calls out in Hebrew, "Welcome!" He's an Israeli from Teheran's Israeli diplomatic mission. He guides us to a taxi and directs the driver to the Kings Hotel, which will be our. temporary new home.

Right away I take up my duties at the Israeli school. The teachers and staff are Israeli, and we speak Hebrew among us. Experienced with the demands of my job, I can quickly take charge and enjoy my work. Initially, the school feels like an oasis of comfort and familiarity where I shelter for a few hours a day from the unfamiliar and confusing outside world where I must master many new skills to make a home for my family. If I wanted to change and challenges, I've found them in Teheran.

Life in Teheran invigorates us. Soon what was strange and intimidating becomes familiar. We have a new home; the children enjoy school and make friends. Ya'akov finds a job he enjoys. He and I study Persian three times a week at the American-Iranian Society not far from our home. I already know enough Persian to haggle with the peddlers in the market and give our maid instructions for preparing two of the daily meals. I've become familiar with our neighbourhood and can comfortably handle our car in Teheran's chaotic streets.

As the school year ends, we feel at home in the Teheran's Israeli community. We've celebrated the Passover Seder with new Israeli friends, and the Israeli school has hosted a celebration of Israel's 30th Independence Day for the whole Israeli community. We feel vital, happy and enjoy our life in Teheran.

Teheran, autumn 1978

Once the new school year begins, the many Israelis in Teheran who've gladly ignored the political struggle between supporters of the Shah's and those of the Ayatollah Khamenei can no longer do so. Now the gas stations are short of fuel; the grocery stores poorly stocked, and there are frequent power outages. Then a curfew is announced. Tanks rumble in the city streets. Smoke rises here and there from explosions around the city. A sense of fear pervades...

One morning, soldiers from Khamenei's revolutionary forces attempt to break down the door to the Israeli school. The school's few Israeli security guards, together with local police, prevent their entry. Teachers and staff members quickly shepherd the frightened children to safety.

Tammi, forced to wear the chador, the headscarf that was compulsory towards the end of their stay in Teheran.

The school staff considers moving classes to the Israeli diplomatic mission. But Khamenei's followers are openly hostile toward Israel, so there's a risk they will attack the mission. Instead, we apportion the children among the school's teachers, who conduct classes for the students in their homes. Meanwhile, our diplomatic duties urge Israeli mothers and children return to Israel. By the eve of Hanukah, Teheran's Israeli community has shrunk to less than a quarter of what it was. The

Israeli school's directors then instruct the school's remaining teachers to take their children back to Israel for "the Hanukah vacation." I pack a couple of suitcases and fly to Israel with Dror and Tammy. Ya'akov stays on with a few others to "wait out the events." After Hanukah, flights between Teheran and Israel cancelled. The Ayatollah's Islamic Revolution has succeeded. Israel is now Iran's arch enemy. Ya'akov escapes on one of the last flights from Teheran to Israel.

Haifa, January 1979

 Our Teheran adventure is over. At age 40, Ya'akov and I suddenly find ourselves back in Israel, empty-handed-without jobs, home or minimal belongings. We must rebuild our lives from scratch. The Israeli school in Teheran has agreed to pay my salary through the current school year, so at least we are not destitute. But this sudden change of fortune leaves us feeling as if all the wind in our sails ceased. Fortunately, we are not without friends, who help us move into a small flat in Haifa. They collect clothing for us and the children, utensils and furniture for the house.

A Clock and mat are all the belongings that remain from a life in Teheran.

They assist us to resettle the children in school and offer encouragement. Even so, for a long time, I feel mentally and physically immobilized, lacking the will to go forward. If there has ever been a pivotal moment in my life, this must be it.

One friend, in particular, refuses to give up on me. Every morning, she appears and prods me to get out of bed, get dressed and rejoin the living. Her gentle persistence slowly revives my life force and helps me regain my perspective. Gradually I can appreciate that I've been very fortunate—for the unique experience of living in Teheran for even a short time, but also because I escaped safely with my family before calamity befell that city. I also remember that I have talents and training and experience from earlier periods of my life to fall back on now as I build my new life. I begin to look around me and soon see a small ad in the newspaper: the Kaduri Elementary School for the Lower Galilee Region is looking for a new principal. At the job interview, the head of the Regional Council gives me an enthusiastic reception, and the job offer follows. In the autumn, I take up my new job, get to know the teachers and staff, and soon am happily engaged in my satisfying new life.

Tivon, Israel August 2017

Since that pivotal moment of my life, I've undertaken additional academic studies and other demanding jobs in the Israeli educational system. Now in retirement, I continue to learn and to be active in socially oriented volunteer work. Challenging moments and ups and downs are part of life at every stage, but the moment I've described here still stands out above the others.

Amira Ben Mor – Kiryat Tivon, Israel

I dedicate this chapter with love to my children Yuval, Dror and Tammi.

Transformation #26

Gratitude for Life

"Women are like Teabags; You don't know how strong they are until you put them in hot water." Eleanor Roosevelt

In 1992, I was a young Mum age 25 with three-year-old twins; life had to be incredibly organised to make every day work. By that I mean I was holding down a management job in a family business. My husband (a builder) and I had just moved into our dream home after living four years on site in a caravan. I was juggling work, kids cooking washing ironing cleaning. I was no different to any mum, life was busy and you just do it.

Until 29 June 1992, my routine before I left the office I rang home to say, "I will be home in 20 minutes" I left dashing across the car park as it had started to rain. A mile down the road the heavens exploded, you know the rain where your wipers are on fast speed, and it still doesn't clear the screen. As I rounded a corner, it felt as if the wheels on my car had locked and I could not steer. I recalled my husband's words "If the car ever slides, steer oppositely" I was frantically pulling the steering wheel, but nothing was happening. Suddenly, there was a tree right in front of me. I braked hard and said to myself "Hold on it will be over in a minute" everything went black.

My car had hit a tree right in the middle of the bonnet, the floor went down, the roof went up, and I felt like the filling in a sandwiched. The fire brigade had to cut me out. I was transported to a hospital in an ambulance while drifting in and out of consciousness.

Once in the emergency room at the hospital, I recall the doctor shining a light in my eyes and I could hear him say he wanted more X-rays on my head. Then suddenly I felt as if I had slipped out through the top of my head. I felt calm and relaxed. I was going toward a bright light in the corner of the room. Looking back, I could see the doctor and nurses around me, and I could see myself lying on the table. Despite, looking a mess, I started drifting towards the light; it was the most wonderful feeling I had ever had in my life.

There are not any words to describe how tranquil, serene and calm I felt, much deeper than any meditation. Then I stopped again and thought of my children, suddenly, I saw my husband arrive in the room. Oh dear, what will he say about his lovely sports car I have crashed. I watched as he walked over and took my hand. He said "don't worry about the car" suddenly in one quick whoosh I was back in my body.

The extent of my injuries was:
Broken Foot
Smashed Ankle
Broken Kneecap
Cracked Pelvis
2 Broken Ribs
Cracked Breast Bone
Lacerations on my neck from the seat belt
Left-hand side of my face; detached from the gum
Skull Fractured in 2 places.

The following few weeks and months were a blur as I tried desperately to come to terms with the trauma in my body. By September the plaster was removed from my leg, on the day the doctor told me I might be able to walk without a stick but not without a limp. I could feel a red mist descend upon me. I refused to listen and took on the gruesome exercises that were so painful. I was determined to get back to myself again. In honesty, it was a couple of years to manage the physical pain and then another couple of years to get over the trauma and emotional stress. There were times that I wished I could just go to that beautiful light again and sometimes I seemed to just slip out of my body for brief moments.

Then three days before my 30th Birthday December 1996 I was diagnosed with cervical cancer. Another shock! The doctor told me that they would do a complete hysterectomy to remove all cancer, but they would not be sure that after ten years I would not take Breast Cancer with the HRT treatment. 2 days after surgery my husband leaned over me and asked how I was feeling. I was getting morphine in one arm and blood in the other. I replied, "I am going to open a Ladies Boutique," he thought I was hallucinating. As I had lain in the hospital bed, I realised I could be a victim of everything that had happened to me, or I could rise. I chose to grow, I was going to shift my focus, don't get me wrong I was grateful to be alive after the car accident, but this time it was different a strength was rising within. I vowed that if I could spend the next ten years with my children, I would create financial security for them, that if I died in 10 years, they would have enough money to be secure for the rest of their lives.

By September 1997 I opened my first business a Ladies Boutique a new creation that gives me a purpose and connection with other women. Within a year I started buying property. I wanted to have a million pound on the property by the time I was 40 years old. Being incredibly focused on my children and my business, within five years I had 1 million. Over the next seven years, I built a multi-million pound portfolio.

My children are now 27. I realise the legacy of money was not the most important, what was most important was what I taught them, to value themselves, live their dreams and treat others with respect.

I am delighted to say I am cancer free. Today, my life is so blessed than the episodes of turmoil and challenge of the last twenty years.

My message to you is your darkest days are your greatest gifts by that I mean in your darkest hour when you don't know the way forward and you feeel broken not knowing where to turn; take a deep breath, be still and look within, the unierse will never give you anuthing you cnnot handle. From here you will grow and become a better stronger you. Remember you hae to be broken to let the light shine through.

Roslyn Bell – Armagh, N.Ireland

I dedicate this chapter to my wonderful children Graham & Lindsey. You are the love of my life and I feel so privileged to have shared your journey of life this far & very proud of who you both have become. Love you both always Mum x

The Art of Feminine Beauty

Vulnerability

Bethany Rivett-Carnac

RESURGE EX CINERIBUS

Transformation #27

Finding Me

"You are not too broken, too scarred or too far gone to change...
Change your thoughts and you can change your world"

The following chapter is my story of hope and inspiration. I desire to encourage women to move forward to live life not just for others but you too.

When my brother was murdered just three weeks before I married as tragic and desperate as this was, it changed mine, and my families' lives forever.

The brother, son, nephew, cousin, friend, fiancé taken so abruptly and tragically and the funny, witty character torn from our lives left us all devastated. The shock was something so consuming I thought life was going to end for us all. Constantly worrying and panicking about all my family kept me awake for a very long time to come, always dreading the telephone ringing at unusual hours.

Living with terror and fear created an overwhelming sense trepidation and panic. How would my mam and dad survive this ordeal? Who would look after my younger brothers and sister? Would my wedding even go ahead?

I left this in the hands of my parents who both had very different views; my mam felt she was losing a second child, and my dad wanted us to go ahead as planned. I think deep down he knew how much more challenging it would have been for me to go ahead at a later stage.

I know from that moment getting the call and arriving at the hospital, and then the heartbreak of having to tell my brothers and sister and calling around family, my instinct, being the oldest at home, was to take care of everyone; I don't think I cared either way.

It wasn't until sometime later I realised despite my family and friends I felt alone in my relationship with my husband. In a short space of time, I lost my brother, married, moved out and transferred to the other side of the city at only 23 years of age. I had a fairy-tale image of how life would be with my husband by my side supporting each other and the hope that one day we would have children; our own little family.

I'm not sure how soon afterwards I realised I had no idea how to be in this kind of relationship and neither did my husband. It wasn't until the day our second daughter was born six years later that I realised just how alone and miserable I felt, at what was supposed to be one of the best moments of your life giving birth to a beautiful, healthy baby girl and feeling so alone. I was surrounded by family and friends and yet alone in my thoughts and unhappiness and felt like I was going crazy

I tried to hide from the outside world just how desperate and unhappy I felt, so no one knew. To our friends, family and neighbours, we had it all, a nice home, decent cars and holidays every year. I was always running away from reality.

After two years of undiagnosed, untreated postnatal depression, I walked out of a job after eleven years and slowly started asking why what was life all about. No matter what I did or what I bought or where I went I wasn't happy. I was looking to the world, to possessions to other people rather than looking at me.

Then the realisation of discovering that my husband, who rarely drank when I met him, was secretly drinking. It was just too much to take especially not knowing how he would be when I came home. At this stage, we both tried to seek help, and I thought, hoped and wanted to believe that things could change and change for the better. I think I knew deep down this wasn't to be.

Over the years I wondered what would happen if I adopted a 'can't beat him join him' attitude. The dilemma was a confusing and self-destructing way of thinking and the cause of my real problems with weight. Consequently, I began to take refuge and comfort in eating and drinking to cope with daily life. I always felt I was the bigger of my friends and this belief transformed into a self-fulling prophecy. I allowed this weight gain to happen to me and it just made me more miserable.

After many new years of talking about change but things never changing my pivotal moment came on New Year's Eve 2006. I knew enough was enough and when he arrived home from work that day I told him I'd had enough and wasn't happy and didn't want our daughters to think this illusion was how a happy couple/parents behaved, this was not a happy home, and I wanted to be happy too. Initially being with two daughters aged six and nine, I felt empowered by the desire and drive to have a better life emotionally and physically too, although this didn't come until sometime later.

The following year or two continued with the help and support of self-help groups, counselling and being honest with my family and friends about how I felt....some come and gone, and I believe that's to be as some people don't like when we change if they aren't getting the same from you.

In May 2010 was when I finally faced my battle with my weight. Slimming world was relatively new in Ireland, and I was blown away by how this healthy lifestyle worked and started seeing results right away. By the time my brother's wedding came around in July, I was already down one stone. Six months later on 1st November 2010, I opened my first Slimming World group, helping others on their journey. I've gone on to lose almost four stone and have maintained my weight loss for over five years. I am now running three successful Slimming world franchises in Co Kildare in Newbridge and Leixlip. Inspiring, motivating, supporting and helping women and men to lose weight and I love it.

Believe in you, change is hard but staying the same is even more of a challenge. You can change despite how you may be conditioned, brought up or what society preaches. Look within; you'll find all your answers, and you are worth it!

Barbara Byrne – Dublin, Ireland

I dedicate this chapter to my parents and my two strong independent daughters for whom I will never give up trying.

RESURGE EX CINERIBUS

Transformation #28

When the Universe Showed Me the Way

"Not only is another world possible, she is on her way.
On a quiet day, I can hear her breathing."

Arundhati Roy, Indian writer.

To say that I spent my life looking for that 'perfect job' is the understatement of the year. My working life has seen me join many a company, industry and sector, searching for that belonging, my exact purpose on this planet. To me, those people who found their dream job or knew what they wanted to do from the outset or childhood, were ones with which I couldn't empathise. I could only wonder when I was going to experience those feelings of finding that 'thing' which is intended for me and me for it. My lack of a dream career or job didn't stop me from living my life, and I grabbed opportunities to travel and work. However, I am always looking, wanting that 'thing', [mostly for me defined by career] something which evoked passion. That was missing from my world.

My pivotal moment came in April 2016. For many years I had wanted to tour South America, and since 2015 especially Peru, but something always got in the way. Fear, mostly and other people's fearful opinions about how it wasn't safe for me to travel on my own.

Now the decision was made though, to go on a once in a lifetime trip to Peru. A company I came across on Facebook looked the perfect company. They organised trips to Peru which looked amazing. A friend of a friend was going on one of their trips soon. And everything about it sounded out of this world. I said to my partner,

'These are the people I want to go with; this looks amazing'.

Speaking to the company to find out further details, the more I knew, the more excitement grew! Following them on social media, I noticed they had a one day workshop coming up 'Introduction to Shamanism' being held only twenty five minutes from my home. There was nothing staggering on the cost front. My inner voice said,

'What have you got to lose, book it, go along and see what it's all about." That's what I did.

That April day arrived & off to Marlow I went. It was experiential workshop learning about shamanic practices & healing tools billed to raise my energetic vibration. It turned out to be fun and exciting. After the course, we made a large fire and a despatcho, [a prayer of gratitude]. Participating in this experience is where it all began. Throughout the day, I felt incredibly spacey, away with the fairies, so to speak, more so than ever before. Once finished, the lady running the workshop offered us all an opportunity to join her training programme, the Medicine Wheel. Experiencing and practicing powerful healing tools of the Inca tradition. [The training to become a Shaman]. It sounded interesting, but I didn't want to commit to a long course with an expensive investment.

Over the next few days, something very unusual happened. I felt a sensation which I can only describe as someone grabbing the front of my top/the collar of my clothes and pulling me forward.

I called the lady who ran the workshop, and she said,

'Oh yes, you've had a call to do the work'.

Overwhelmed was an understatement! I knew that all of me had wanted to do this and yet how was it going to happen. I hadn't planned for a significant investment of time and money. I remembered this lady sharing her story when she had a call to do the work and how she had to travel to America, leaving her family and her business, she merely begun by saying 'YES'.

All decisions before this had been mindless ideas I'd thought about, often analysed for a long time and there was no physical sensations or nothing like the emotions I had experienced in this situation. It was a real lesson for me; when the universe wants you to do something, it shows you and aligns everything to make it happen. And that is what happened for me.

So I said, "Yes," to what I now call a divine, holy yes; words which I hadn't known or uttered previously. After saying yes, and receiving the information about the course. I realised the timing of the second module was when I was travelling to Iceland with my partner. We were extending his work trip. He had recently bought me a business class ticket. I contacted the company and told them that there's no way I can do this. Brian has just bought me this ticket; I couldn't say to him, "Sod you, I'm off to do my own thing." It's rude and naturally doesn't sit right with me.

Now I had been told I had a calling and I knew the universe shows you a way. In the next few days, my partner said to me,

'Iceland might be off.' Brian informed me.

'What, what do you mean?' I asked in surprise.

'Work is cancelling all non-urgent travel!' he replied.

Low and behold, the trip was cancelled and so had a free pass to go and do the training.

The training was intensive, four modules over eight months. My holy 'Yes' meant I'd surrendered to my gut feeling that this course is intended for me. I didn't have a clue what I had signed up for when I wrote my name for the class and said that holy yes. Many days are lasting 12-15 hours, encompassed my healing journey and learned powerful healing practices to use with clients that would help them through issues they had in their life.

The transformation took place, particularly my relationships with my family and partner. I am aware of how I impacted those relationships previously often negatively. After years of muddling through I've made positive changes and my relationships are now better than ever.

Learning that I am in control of my destiny and that I am capable of having and achieving anything I want is freeing. Yes sometimes the universe switches things up a bit, and it's not exactly as I imagine it's going to be. I know I don't want to experience this life as things 'happening to me', but rather I am creating the life that I design. Having this personal control is very important to me. Being the creator of my life is a substantial change for me. It is powerful to know that whatever life throws at me, I can deal with it and that the universe has my back. My intuition and my body are the biggest guides, not just my mind.

Now I can help others to see that they can change their lives too and that is so rewarding, and I'm eternally grateful for that. I know this is just the beginning and the work that I do with women is going to continue for many years even though I haven't got a 20-year plan! I don't need to know, everything only follow the holy yes' follow the path which calls and step away from the rest.

Lucy Tobias - UK

I dedicate this chapter to my partner and my family because I'm blessed to have them in my life.

RESURGE EX CINERIBUS

The Art of Feminine Beauty

Walking the Great Wall of China for Cancer

Roslyn Bell is a strong, courageous and determined woman. As a Pivotal Moment 101 woman who has transformed her life she knows the secret of her success is by helping others.

As a cancer survivor she walked the Great Wall of China for MacMillan Cancer to mark her 50th birthday and being 20 years free from cancer. *Roslyn Bell*

Transformation #29

Breaking Open

"She is a searcher of her own soul; a seeker of her own joy; a discoverer of her own light; finally a friend to her own heart."

C. S. Lourie

Here I am writing from the comfort of my bed. I feel an open space around me, free to be. The density of the air is light. The thoughts in my mind are without judgement. The emotions in my heart are truly mine, without refrain. It's interesting that I use the description "comfort" with where I am sitting now because my life was NOT so comfortable before.

Behind the scenes, we had a LOT of turmoil and stress. And it had grown year over year. My husband's job was extremely demanding, and he all too often made work the priority and spent more time away on work travel than at home. When he first started his trips, my youngest was only four weeks old. I cried when I gave him the goodbye hug as he left for his journey, worried about how I'd make it solo for those 4-7 days. But after several practices as a solo parent, my skin toughened, and I figured out a routine. I was all right without him. The girls and I got along in our rhythm.

It was a lie. On the outside, however, everyone still viewed us as an attractive couple; Gorgeous family; Happy and helpful spirits; Having beautiful things and good jobs; and a Comfortable lifestyle.

I reached out to incorporate another element into our lives with the intent of it balancing me out, giving me right stimulation, and it provides more for our family financially. I took on entrepreneurship. My mind did grow. My belief in my abilities grew. I bought into my dreams 100%. Riding the roller coaster of this endeavour was thrilling really. My mind was expanding yet my husband's mind was not. We had critical discussions more than supportive ones. I felt the gifts of owning a business would be the benefits returned from the initial years of hard work needed for success. I desired abundance in all forms because I believed it to be possible.

My days were now full with managing many elements, all to make others ultimately happy. I subconsciously maintained the "status quo" image of our family. Inside I was dying. I was not living a transparent life. My heart just ached for support and love. The quiet space around me seemed SO loud than previously aware! Now, I was twirling in a tornado of negative vibrations. These angry voices criticized my doings; confusion and frustration that my daughter, who didn't know how to navigate her anxieties, resulted in her hitting, biting and yelling at her sister and myself. A fake image I maintained because I felt shame in openly sharing my truth.

I can see the hallway now from where I am sitting telling you my story. Here is where I collapsed. I described my life like a tornado. And one day as I was holding my daughter's door closed shut as to prevent her from attacking me and or my youngest daughter due to a tantrum she was in; my strength gave way. I was pulling and pulling on the door to keep the resistance. As much as I was holding my tears back from the pain of being in another episode, they came flooding thru and starting streaming down my face. My body began to shake. And I began to call out to a higher power, "Help! Please help me! Please help my Daughter! I can't do this alone ANYMORE!" It was as if a reactive force came thru for me to cry out this plea. My body broke - I collapsed on the floor, sobbing uncontrollably in a pile of tears!

I don't even remember what happened to my daughters. It's as if the whole setting froze with an instant calmness. Everything except me, praying out these words over and over; I invited in The Divine, my Lord. I surrendered. I pleaded for guidance and support.

My prayer was the start of it. Surrendering was the pivotal moment that brought me to grace, authenticity and peace in my heart. I invited in what I now know as the infinite and unwavering embrace that is consistently available to me...for you...for us.

I began to open doors that I wouldn't have done before because it was a "no-no". I spoke truths about what wasn't serving me in my marriage; I advocated for particular care or different modalities that could potentially help my daughter; I stood firm about my business and personal development being good for my soul. Standing up for me with a knowing that I acquired from tuning into the Divine, and my higher self, brought so much reward.

I had this unwavering faith in being vulnerable. The Divine gave me the courage to walk a path that I didn't necessarily know where it was taking me. I felt supported thru some tough conversations. And each time I used my strength, beauty was revealed on the other side. What was this beauty? It's a soul satisfaction that I was honouring myself and becoming more in alignment to feel happiness and love. All was done and walked with so much unconditional love. The Divine made this very clear. That while I was honouring ME, I was also very loving and compassionate to the others involved. It is this grace that the Divine will guide anyone to happiness and peace in their heart. This faith became both my fuel and my safety net. I knew I was being supported 100% to come into a life that served me which would then allow me to assist my family and the collective around me in the way designed for me.

The pivotal moment I first had brought more pivotal moments. And at every moment of "enough is enough" we have a choice. We have an opportunity to come more into our authentic selves or to hide or compromise. And I am here to encourage others to use their courage, to ask for Divine support and to walk with this faith because it IS worth it!

I would like to share a journal entry with you. It's a raw moment. My words describe an emotional experience of me facing myself- and having a dialogue about if I was letting fear and doubt (my ego side) lead my life or if it was Divine guidance. Awakening this awareness came after having many heartfelt conversations with my husband which led to our separation. And I hope that you can listen to it and feel how one of your personal experiences, perhaps, could be applied.

I lay here feeling spent. I feel like my heart, and my mind twisted around one another and then put thru the wringer, shook out then tossed aside. My figure has simply melted down into a sloppy pile. Life is starting to come back though. I had a good cry. As much as I dislike this emotional drain, I also feel renewed, and so I embrace it the same.

In this space, I find the quiet moment now for the energy to twitch back thru my body to reassure it again. I know I will be standing tall again soon.

It's just these fucking draining moments bring me to an inner quarrel. The quarrel has to happen though. My moment of despair is when I face my God. I feel that I've been following the Divine path; I see a sign and follow; I see another sign so turn to support that. I know I've done it over and over. And I've felt the courage to do it. I've walked in trust...

As I begin to breathe slowly again, I'm able to confirm it hasn't been my ego toying with me. I truly have been following the Divine path. I have been prudent and noticed the right signs.

This quarrel just gives me a chance to recalibrate. The exhaustion made me weak. Everything was wrung out except for the single most sustaining aspect. And that is the breath. The pulsing inspiration of the Spirit I felt caresses my body. And the breath is Spirit, not ego. As my form lay there, I knew its revival seemed possible with Spirit. And it had been revived! This and self-love is all I need. It's all going to be ok. I'm rising from my melted pile, allowing the pulses of energy and breaths of Divine Spirit to fill me.

For me now, I can curl up in this bed feeling so nourished by my day. I can look around and feel grateful for all of the turmoil, for sharing all of the secrets in my closet, and for sharing my voice. I feel FREE! I can climb in with a certain satisfaction about my future and with contentment on my heart. And, you deserve the same! You will still walk thru the fire, but, you will be okay. You'll be more than fine! Your heart will begin to tell you how incredible this is. The deep dives you end up taking with the Divine will allow your soul to SHINE truly!

Erron Noel – Colorado, USA

I dedicate this chapter to Billy, who for all those 17years loved me, taught me and exposed me to many facets of life that enhanced my character and adorned me with poise. We came to our breaking moment though. But I see that as a gift now. It transformed me and is allowing me to come into the truest version of myself. And I pray that our uncoupling will become the biggest catalyst for you as well so that you may live the most fulfilled soul satisfying experience too! With so much unconditional love, Erron.

Transformation #30

Forgiveness Means Letting Go

'Our glory is not in never falling, but getting up every time we do'

Confucius

I have always loved this quote, one of many that resonate with me deeply; a kind of mantra which I have lived by; and its impact encouraged me to take up Martial Arts for many years. I am retired now from the sport I initially took up to improve my confidence so I could test myself with experiences I'd never thought I could do. My success has proven just how far I have grown, and continue to learn about myself - indeed, getting knocked down eight times means rising nine. I will never give up, and I don't want you to give up either, whatever your background; if I can do it, you can too.

My story starts early in life and though I suffered emotional and physical abuse from my father I believed I had a relatively 'acceptable' childhood, mainly because I lived in a place that was leafy, woody and rural. There, I could escape into the world that was imaginative and creative. Nature saved me; it was a beautiful world. This world was opposed to the darkness I felt in my home life. The father who should have been my protector became everything that would be an anathema to me. Everything seemed heightened because I am an only child where the focus is entirely on me. Consequently, I had to develop and learn quickly distinct mechanisms to cope with my crazy darkness.

Those who have been through abuse may understand detachment and denial; these strategies meant I could function daily and see my unusual experiences as a typical part of growing up. My saving grace was my incredible Imagination. Although my internal world was dark and scary, it was also bright and beautiful because I made it so. I felt an old soul in a young body, and I was a natural artist who could express that feeling world on paper; I dealt with the pain by escaping. I knew nature was alive; I understood I wasn't alone; the world was multi layered and colourful as were my dreams and nightmares.

I understood as a natural part of life that somewhere deep in my soul I was on a path, and I would be ok. However, as I grew up, that darkness and pain became increasingly a part of my life as the enormity of what happened grew as I did; the darkness was overwhelming. Experiencing loving relationships, which should have been a natural part of maturity, became insidious, painful and torturous because I wouldn't allow anyone in or become close to me. I lived within this prison of pain for many years and one day it dawned on me; I had to change my life.

Although I had the incredible support of my husband at the time, counselling was my 'fix' for years, and this darkness burned like a poker in my soul; my heart broken in pieces, and I cried internally for all that had happened. The tears I shed reflected an inner child who was alone and fearful of what was around the corner. I blamed myself, I hated myself, and I was fractured too deeply to comprehend. It felt like I was walking in a thick fog from which I could never escape. Sadly, my marriage ended for lots of reasons; it had taught me insightful lessons about myself.

My Pivotal Moment was the day I ***allowed*** my prison doors to open, I can't explain why or when this happened, but I forgave myself, and

I forgave my dad, I felt suddenly unshackled from shame, pain, and guilt.

The impact of my pivotal moment was learning about the power of **forgiveness**, but true forgiveness had to start with loving myself. To accept myself in all its darkness and light, to embrace both these energies is who, and what I am. And that's okay. I'm not perfect. However, the past has made me the person I am today for which I am grateful. I am flawed, a bit loose at the seams, yet a person who can empathise with other people's pain, and now help others on their journey to find themselves.

My Pivotal Moment taught me that I cannot change what happened, but I have a **choice** and power to work with the past in a positive way that extends beyond me. I have forgiven my father, something I never thought was possible. By shifting my mindset I released those shackles I speak of, it was truly a memorable day when I woke up and realised, however cliché it sounds, I feel forgiveness, which was heartfelt, from my soul; from the deepest part of me, which is sacred. It had taken a long time to get to that point.

I recognise I still carry the wounds and scars of my past but releasing the pain for me was part of bringing love back into my being which has been my greatest healer.

I end with these words of wisdom that even though I was knocked down many times, I always get up again which has always been the mantra in my life. I still marvel at the beauty and healing power of human beings, we all have the ability to turn our own lives around if we chose to, however dark it may seem, we can do it! And I'm just a 'normal' person like you! And I will always be grateful to those who have walked and continue to walk alongside me on this journey. I also extend this love to you, because you can do it too.

Debbie Arthurs – London, UK

I dedicate this chapter to my Loved Ones, the Universe, & Natural World in all its Glory.

The Art of Feminine Beauty

Fire

Lacey Eshleman

RESURGE EX CINERIBUS

Transformation #31

The Power of Decisions

"Women can have it all...be whoever she wants to be...
Without forgetting who she is."

Jurgita Kasparr

December 2010

I checked my balance at the cash point, and it was showing I had 30 pence in my bank account in spite of working full time.

I came to the UK for the second time to try and build my life again after I split up with my partner. I left my children in Lithuania, as I thought I would be visiting for only a few days, as I was coming for a job interview.

To my surprise, I had to start immediately within a few days, if I wanted the job.

Eight months passed before I would see my children again. My heart was breaking every time I saw my kids on Skype, and at one point I even stopped calling them for about a month as I could not bear to see the sad eyes of my little boys or hear their voices.

I believed I have no choice!

I thought I must work in a job I hate; I must become invisible, blend in, pay my bills, hide my beauty, my feminine desires and just accept what life has in store for me. Somehow I had been told by someone that people don't like beautiful and successful women. I did not want to become that perfect bitch that has it all, so I decided to blend in instead. I became a slave of my own life.

I became invisible and unhappy. I was feeling guilty for being beautiful, sexy and intelligent at the same time as I mistakingly did not want to give a perfect reason to be hated.

That December was cold, and it was snowing so badly, I have never seen so much snow here in London. The memory is vivid for I had to walk for more than two hours to and from work because I could not afford a bus ticket. I could not afford food. I could not afford to dream.

I felt so humiliated, upset and angry. I could not understand why I was in this desperate predicament. Why did it happen to me; a person who is well educated, loving, friendly, and hard working? I was broke not only financially, but I was also broken as a woman, as a person and as a mother who was not able to look after own children. I could not even help myself!

Just before Christmas, I became ill; a complicated form of flu that I should have called an ambulance, but at that moment, the only thing that was going through my mind while lying in bed; "I must pull myself together as I have to go to work!"

Pain and disappointment were slicing my whole body. That was my breaking point. When I could not handle that pain; I promised myself I would never allow myself or anybody else to treat me like I am worthless and a 'nothing'. I understood, of course, I will have to change how I think, how I behave. I will have to change my environment and most importantly - how I treat myself.

I think that was one of the scariest moments, but to stay here and in such situation, was scarier, and I could not remain in that desolate place anymore. I never went back to my old job.

Within few months I was working for a new company, being recognised for my efforts. I was driving my car. My children and I moved into our home, and suddenly everyone started calling me a 'lucky' woman and saying how easy it was for me always to get what I want.

It took years to change many things, I had to make many mistakes, I had to let go of some people from my life, and I had to let go many habits that were not helping me. I had to learn how to love and respect myself. I wanted to fall in love with myself. I wanted to be turned on by myself. I wanted to feel sexy and beautiful again and not be ashamed of it; EVER!

I had to learn how to love and respect money. I had to find out how to receive money and be comfortable with having money in my life. I had to grasp how to love and respect men. I had to know how to accept from males without manipulating them or feeling guilty. The male species are remarkable, and they treat us like Queens if we allow them to do so.

I had to take responsibility for my own life, build strong boundaries in my life and stop playing the victim. I had to stop judging others and MYSELF! I had to learn not to shrink if I thought I could outshine someone. I had to accept that it is natural to know what I desire and request it.

It took many years to understand and accept myself, treating myself with joy and pride EVERY SINGLE DAY, but it took only a moment to make that decision. I had to make the decision that I am ready for a transformation no matter what.

I am deserving.   I am worthy.

I am good enough.   So are You.

My reasons are not to motivate as I don't believe in motivation. My reasons are to remind myself how important it is to set boundaries; how important it is not to go into a compromise with myself and also to connect YOU, my reader. I urge you to get to know your deepest strength so you can acknowledge and claim your self-worth without feeling guilty of being beautiful, loving, successful, sexy, feminine and happy.

These qualities are not a weakness; they are your strength. In acknowledging and accepting these divine qualities, you will find love and success. It is time to come out from the shadows and take control of all you desire.

All it takes is a moment when you decide to claim your worth back and do not accept anything, under no circumstances, that are not serving you anymore. Make the decision that you will be the most important person in your own life. Decide that your life is the most important for you. Identify your non-negotiables and stick by those decisions, so you will be and do what makes your life a better place for yourself and others.

I want you to become The Woman who has freedom, money, love and self-worth; who becomes the Queen of her own life.

Jurgita Kasparr

I dedicate this chapter to all my loving family, my amazing friends who support and believe in me no matter what. I also dedicate this story to everyone who came into my life. I want to say a big thank you to my sons, Klaidas and Kernius that they chose me as their mother and I am honoured every day to experience what it means to experience the unconditional

mother's love.

Transformation #32

Everything is possible

"You get what you have the courage to ask for."

Oprah Winfrey

I would love to start my little story by telling you I had a very happy childhood. I loved to be around the kids and as the oldest in my family, most of the time I was a leader in the games. I was confident; I loved the stage and the limelight.

Everything started to change at school.

I remember the first event when I had the biggest lesson in my life "To keep my mouth shut". During the break time, we played "hide and seek" a favourite childhood game. One boy hid in the bushes, and I knew it. Nobody could find him, and he was the last one to be found. As the break was about to end, I told my friends where they could find him. Divulging his whereabouts incensed him that he ran straight from the bushes towards to me and kicked me so painfully. From that day I was so scared of him, that I decided to go to another class. I didn't say anything to my parents or my sisters about this event; I kept it to myself. My parents supported my decision to go to another class, but I can't remember what I said to them, not the reason for the change.

In my new class I was much happier, but started to have another challenge – I am not the leader! I wasn't good enough to be a leader! I was doing my best always, but I still felt not good enough!

My grandma believed in me, and I felt I had to keep proving this to her. I know that she loved me, kept spoiling me, she was proud of me and I couldn't disappoint her. Did I? I was doing my best to keep her being proud of me. My limiting decision of "not good enough" became very intense and a large part of my life when I became a teenager; a significant period in our lives when we are starting to find ourselves.

Every Sunday, my mum, sisters and I went to the Mass. I loved it. As I still was quite open at that time, I shared with the class: how it made me feel, what the bible teaches us, and so on. Unfortunately, it was at this point that some of my peers started to laugh and keep twitting me. Soon some neighbour's kids started twitting too. As a consequence, every day I was being bullied at school. They called me a nun and the neighbour's children called me a 'prude' (bigot). It distressed me so much; I didn't know what to do or how to stop it. Every night I imagined how the next day I would tell them off; how I will stand up for myself; then when the day comes, I don't have the strength to do it. I was scared.

All hurt transformed into anger. I was angry, furious. I started bullying and abusing my sisters and some neighbour's kids who were smaller than me too.

At that time our little brother was born. He was adorable. I fell in love. He was a miracle. I was ready to do anything for him. Also, we were a family of four kids living in a crisis in Lithuania; my parents were struggling with money. So when my brother was one and a half years old, me (aged13), my mum went back to work, and I was left to look after my brother. After a sleepless night (every 2-3 hours I needed to give him a bottle and rock him) I was taking him to the nursery, then off to my school. Even when I was exhausted, I didn't complain. I saw it as my duty to contribute to our family. To be from a big family and having no money was another reason for others to bully me.

There is another significant event which affected my life; this took place in the swimming pool. I went with few of my class friends to swim, and at the same time, there were teenagers from the children's shelter. While we were swimming about ten of them swam closer to me and started touching my body. I was terrified; I couldn't escape. Their teachers didn't look like they cared; only my friends came and shouted at them to leave me alone. I couldn't tell my parents what happened, so I just put myself even more into the shell in which I was already hiding. The consequences of this event meant that for many years, I was scared to even to stay with my dad on my own; I didn't want to have any men close to me.

All of these traumatic events resulted in me spuriously learning that I am not good enough; to keep my mouth shut, and don't trust people. I hated my life. It was just a huge pain. I knew (that's what I learned) that God loves those who are suffering in their lives, but it was too much. It was getting worse and worse: more bullying, more hurt and anger. I couldn't handle it anymore, then one day I find myself standing on the window ledge; I was standing and thinking whether to jump or not?

Today I am so happy and grateful that at that moment I decided to stay. God heard my prayers, and my life became beautiful. People accepted me and helped me to grow spiritually. I started focusing on my goals to prove, that I am good enough. At the time, I didn't know that visualisations can help you to reach your goals, but I am doing it (it was God's present to me). Before going to sleep, I imagine that I am a nurse, that I am working in the hospital, I have a wonderful husband, and we have an amazing life. Guess what? My final national exam was the best in our school. I finished my nursing bachelor degree and public health management master degree. I am happily married to an amazing man whom I love so much, we have two lovely daughters, and now I run a coaching business helping women to see what they are worth. It has become my mission to show women all the power they have in themselves - because I promise - you do have it too - so you can excel in your life and your dreams.

Rita Grineviciene – Lithuanian living in Peterborough, UK

I dedicate this chapter to my loving grandmother.

The Art of Feminine Beauty

Small Hours

In the small hours of the morning
I contemplate my life and
all the while it is getting there,
yet something fails to feel quite right.

There is something stuck inside me,
the words to express it just can't find me.
I can't prove it to anyone, and I must
let my feelings deny me.

I feel it pushing me,
but it also deprives me.
It's sure alive and kicking me
its cross I bear that is sickening me.

It always called me; would show
proof of its existence, when laughed at
and judged in an instant. I turned sceptic
just ignored instincts to fit in and be accepted,

Many foes surround me with their fears
who dare to doubt me but my many friends
shine throughout me. I'm enlightened but
still sad, alone and frightened.

The discoveries within me see
it has no beginning, no end.
All of my worst fears and doubts
have become my biggest friends.

They make sense of our world and
in my time spent here every new facet
makes the bigger picture so clear.
Mistakes I make, I see in new light.

I look at myself and see cloudiness.
I've missed the point of life;
now lost,
draw inward protected and shrouded.

The rain falls while the clouds part and
the sunshine pours out from within my heart,
a rainbow appears in my sky,
I know I must continue, to do or die.

A Pivotal Moment turns our lives around,
these precious moments in life found
in much silence; we can hear a new sound
of nature, we can let go and learn so much.

Every raindrop, every leaf,
every ripple in the river,
every note in birdsong, within listening
to nature you'll never go wrong.

Drumming a beat in our hearts,
feeling into our bodies for guidance

and writing a new song,
a new story, a brand new day is on its way,

Chin up, chest out, uniqueness and self-love
is what it's all about.
Express your fears and doubts in
Finding yourself as individuals

Take the Leap of Faith and
Know you are safe
in paradise; embrace the sublime
journey to finding yourself.

Willow Sterrick

Transformation #33

The Darkest Hour is just Before Dawn

"A Diamond is simply a piece of charcoal that has undergone immense darkness and pressure."

Brenda Dempsey

Wallowing in self-pity, paralysed by the blight of inactivity and feeling sucked of all energy was the dark world I found myself in.

Darkness I had grown accustomed to over a period of ten years. At first, you don't realise the dark shadow over you. It's clever. There are many times when veiled in light that a little darkness enters the realm. That's okay...for in life there is dark, shade and light. Its sinister nature, however, leads you to a false sense of reality and the length of darkness extends itself before becoming a frequent visitor.

My blackness was living with abuse. It began with the psychological kind; the worst kind. Initially, it was in doors then soon became the 'banter' during social occasions; subtle in its delivery before the torment unleashed paranoia.

Next was the verbal abuse. The cursing, name calling and total belittling that erodes every morsel of your self-belief, self-worth and self-confidence. As this escalated, so too did the physical form of abuse. I was engulfed in darkness the only light being my four children, my family and the time when my husband went to work. A slither of light did come one day when I left my marital home for the last time... or so I thought.

At the time, feeling hopeless, I plunged into an ever darker world. Homeless with four children; depending on friends and family to support me in any way they could, I soon secured a safe house for my kids and me. There was a great sense of relief on the one hand while experiencing the juxtaposition of a sense of despair and disbelief on the other. Nonetheless, I was safe; we were secure.

After a few months, I was rehoused by the council and could carry on with my degree. You see, during this time I was in the final year of my Bachelor of Education degree at university. Here I was a single parent; juggling the day to day living of being a mother to four amazing kids; supporting ill parents daily and studying for my freedom.

A super woman was how I looked to everyone on the outside. "How does she do it?" These were the words on everyone's lips. Unbeknown, I was crashing on the inside. The darkness was growing blacker and blacker. I could no longer see how I could keep it all together. The cracks were growing ever wider; dragged towards a black hole. "Oh God help me!" I implored.

I continued this struggle for six months. I found it more challenging to carry out all of the things I needed to do. I had continued at university, barely managing to complete tasks; always handing everything in at the last minute. But at least I submitted my assignments even if the quality had suffered a little.

They say the darkest hour is just before dawn.

Feeling like I was crawling on my belly, I had hit a brick wall. There were three weeks to go before my final dissertation had to be submitted.

Graduating with a teaching degree was my ticket to freedom. The 'Golden Fleece' I needed to improve our lives. My why, was my children, the driving force to get us out of the dark hole in which we lived. Despite knowing this, my resolve had diminished so much I had nothing left. I felt like I had succumbed to the Darkness. I was its prisoner.

I felt naked on the floor, and the darkness enveloped me in its power. I was done!

One day, as I passed my bedroom, I glanced inside to see my computer and the pile of work sitting for me to sift through and write my ten thousand word dissertation. It was like groundhog day for a few weeks; it had become my habit until I screamed. "Enough is Enough is Enough". What had I become? This once strong woman broken, desperate and in need of a miracle had been struck with a glimmer of light, hope and purpose.

Was I going to let others have the last word? Was I going to give up on my childhood dream of becoming a teacher? Was I going to give up on the opportunity of a better life? NO!

I sat myself down and began sifting through all the research, reading and interviews I had carried out months before. I structured my thesis and started writing the ten thousand words to freedom. With two days to go before the deadline, I finally submitted my Dissertation. WOW, it felt good! The darkness had dissipated during this time; I felt lighter than I had for months, and the smile had returned to my sullen face. There was no turning back. The darkness dispelled from my life for good.

Besides the birth of my four children, my graduation is the happiest, proudest and most fulfilling day of my life. I was walking on air. Nothing and no-one could spoil that feeling. The light was glorious, and I could now see once again. I felt reborn.

Sometimes in life, you are dealt a hand that you would rather not hold. You want to throw it in, reshuffle the pack and trade another set of cards. Who's to know that they will be any better? They could even be worse. It's learning how to play them that's important. Another thing the hand doesn't last forever even though it feels like it at the time.

So what has been the impact of my darkness?

Life changed dramatically for my family and me. With my degree under my belt, I could now work for the first time in years. Not only could I work but be paid well for it too. This financial gain allowed me to improve the quality of my children's lives. We could go places and do things. What's more, I could repay everyone who had been there for me during my darkest times.

The biggest reward was being able to buy my home. Have more financial stability at the same time as doing a job I loved; teaching. My childhood dream realised. I was happy, energised and free. Now, I was ready for my next chapter.

Brenda Dempsey

I dedicate this chapter to my four children in gratitude for their unconditional love. It is fitting that I also dedicate this chapter to all the women who are rising to create a better world for everyone.

RESURGE EX CINERIBUS

Epilogue

After many video calls, excitement and much determination, I sit here in gratitude and humility for the trust that the courageous women who have bared their souls in this Anthology, have given to me.

From the conception of the idea for this Anthology to the final full stop, it has been a great adventure for the human spirit and our souls. In the many conversations with the wonderful co-authors, they have revealed how writing their story has healed them. They have appreciated the opportunity to raise their voice, knowing that their struggle has not been in vain.

As the book came together and an Extract created, it allowed sharing the flavour of these compelling stories with other women. The ripple effect of the stories is the whole point of the book to illustrate how darkness can be the gift that brings light and transformation as well as a profound human connection.

In its very shortened form (Extract) it has been greatly welcomed and appreciated. From reading the stories, women have found the courage to voice their struggles and are now contemplating joining Pivotal Moments 101 – Volume II

Without a shadow of a doubt, from the experience of their challenges, the co-authors intend their story will impact other women and have found inspiration to further their vision and purpose of serving others. Like the symbolic image of the rising Phoenix, these powerful women are soaring and have voiced their transformation and determination from the journey they began as being part of Pivotal Moments 101.

There is more in store for them as they now work beyond the book and 'Voices of Women' will be heard across the globe.

Pivotal Moments 101 has developed into a trilogy, and subsequently, there are plans for launches in London, Paris and New York.

From a simple idea the work of Pivotal Moments 101 –Voices of Women – will travel the world through the book, a Barbados Retreat April 2018 and a Global Woman's Conference in Machu Picchu, Summer 2018.

The new (VOW) 'Voice of Women,' will be heard in the four corners of our world and in so doing will impact on changing the world for the better.

When women work together, they lift each other up to a height beyond human thought and unleash a spirit that leads them home to peace, happiness and love.

RESURGE EX CINERIBUS

It's time to unleash your Inner Diamond

Remember...Leave your Sparkle everywhere you go...

Acknowledgements

I would like to thank all of my fellow courageous co-authors for saying "Yes" to being part of this awesome journey. You are making a significant difference to the world.

I would like to thank David Lakey, my loving partner, who has supported me throughout this new adventure, believing I could achieve my dreams.

There have been a number of people of who have answered questions along the way for which I am eternally grateful.

I would like to thank all the women who encounter pivotal moments every day and who are yet to share their story with the world. Your time will come.

Meet Co-Authors

Transformation #1 - Louize Spittle, Bilbrook, UK

Louize Spittle is a 30-year-old, Business Woman and Mom from Bilbrook, England. She is a Master Practitioner of NLP, Master Practitioner of Hypnotherapy, Master NLP Coach and Master Practitioner of Timeline Therapy. Louize has had a lot of pivotal moments in her life and has now embraced that to help others.
https://www.facebook.com/louize.jackson

Transformation #2 - Dovile Strazdiene, Vilnius, Lithuania

Dovile Strazdiene is an abstract artist, wife and mother of a four-year-old boy, Tim, cancer survivor and optimistic soul. She loves to create colourful paintings, read spiritual books, uplift and inspire others and is a strong believer in miracles. Dovile lives with her lovely family in the beautiful city Vilnius, the capital of Lithuania. Connect with Dovile at: www.dovilestrazdiene.com

Transformation #3 –Gitana Shillin, Berkshire, UK

Gitana (from Lithuania) is a transformational coach helping people to realise that ANYTHING IS POSSIBLE!!! Her passion is to lead others to the discovery of their secret to success and happiness. She lives in Berkshire with her two grown-up children, her partner, crazy dog

and lazy cat. She adores nature, animals, good food and classy shoes. Connect with Gitana at:

www.crushonyourself.co.uk

.Transformation #4 - Lauren Hornby, Walkern, UK

Lauren Elise Hornby works with children and young people and practices energy medicine. She enjoys writing, studying and is particularly interested in looking at alternative ways to work with the kids. Lauren has experience writing academically, including co-authoring an academic journal and hopes to continue writing in the future. She has both a Bachelor's Degree in Early Years and Childhood Studies and is working towards a Master's Degree. She has passion for working with children and young people and supporting them in sharing their gifts with the world. Connect with Lauren at: laurenhornby.shaman@ gmail.com

Transformation #5 - Trina Kavanagh, Nottingham, UK

Trina Kavanagh is a Personal Trainer (Trina at TKT Fitness), Blogger and more recently Founder of Zest Workshops – 4 Steps to a Brighter More Energetic Woman. Her core emphasis is helping women with confidence issues return to fitness. She loves writing and being active with a passion for inspiring more women to become active long-term. She left her city roots 14 years ago and now resides in the beautiful Nottinghamshire UK countryside with three children, three dogs and five ferrets. Connect with Trina at: www.trinakavanagh.co.uk

Transformation #6 - Willow Sterrick, High Wycombe, UK

Willow is an Intuitive Life Coach for women who covers a vast range of guidance from Self-Discovery to coping with and recovery from Mental Health; from relationship issues to spiritual counselling; from Crystal & Sound healing to Shamanic healing; from working with Natures gifts to reveal within, secrets of self yet undiscovered. She is passionate about connecting with the teachings of Mother Earth and all of Nature. From barefoot walking to blue sky dreaming, the essential caring & honouring the natural flora and fauna in our systems and those of the Earth, listening to the winds of inner change, braving the eye of the storm, facing shadows and creating your Rainbows, Sunshine and Magic. Connect with Willow: willlowherbpark396@gmail.com

Transformation #7 – Anita Smith {Hungarian), Lincs, UK

Anita Smith is a freedom seeker, dream follower, a 'No excuses taken' Mindset and Business Coach. She helps girls to transform their lives and business by the power of deep coaching. She found herself called to coaching when her father passed away without realizing his dreams. She has a wonderful hubby and two amazing toddlers. Connect with Anita at: www.youcanmakeyouhappy.com

Transformation #8 - Bonnie Harmon, Hertfordshire, UK

Bonnie is a coach, mentor and businesswoman who works with both individuals and big businesses. She is a former Futures and Options accountant at JP Morgan, and a director of her own £MM business for 12 years, which she co-founded while bringing up her three children. Bonnie has a work

ethic that belies her gentle demeanour. She is also an NLP Master Practitioner, and EFT Master Practitioner, a Master Life Coach, and an Emotional and Social Intelligence Coach, a Social Entrepreneurship Trainer, and a Modern Stress Management Trainer. In a sea of men, she had to carve out her path and discovered how she too could be successful in business and help others to do the same: while not being masculine in her approach but instead through embracing her profound values of integrity, love, and loyalty.
www.businesstransformation.consulting

Transformation #9 - Kate Young, Essex, UK

Kate Young is a 36-year-old coach and entrepreneur. She is a spiritual soul, with a fire in her belly. Kate looks for the best in everyone, even when they can't see it themselves. She will lift you up and inspire you to believe in yourself, helping you see all the beautiful things you have inside to offer the world. Kate wants to empower women to feel strong and secure in themselves, their beliefs and their relationships. She is mum to 2 wonderfully quirky girls and is married to best friend and partner in crime, Ray. She was born and bred in Essex. Connect with Kate: www.facebook.com/kmann69

Transformation #10 - Orit Adiri (Israeli), Nottingham, UK

Orit Adiri is a weight loss maven with a history of an eating disorder. After taking a weight loss course, Orit then researched about healthy nutrition doctrines and combined these with her life-long experiences and created a weight loss programme naturally. As a diamond grader, Orit has a natural eye for the unique quality of her clients. She is a mother of two and lives in Manchester, UK. Connect with Orit at:
https://www.facebook.com/WeighLessLiveMore/

Transformation #11 - Fiona Clark, Redhill, UK

Fiona Clark is a Midlife Empowerment Coach with a compassionate, down-to-earth and holistic approach to healing her customer on a mind, body and spirit level, emerging rewired to their inner power as they embrace the courage to be themselves again. Over the last 25 years, Fiona has studied Kinesiology, Reflexology, Theta Healing and Coaching plus much more and uses many of these techniques with her clients.

Fiona looks at midlife as a time of reinvention; it's an exciting time to focus on ourselves and connect to our inner wisdom. She is a keen cyclist and a single mother of two teenage boys and two cheeky dogs! She lives in Surrey, and you can connect with her at; www.fionaclark.co.uk

Transformation #12 - Alison Watson, Barbados

Alison Watson loves life! Since she discovered her creative talents, Alison has never been the same. She is happier today! Alison is a poet and mother of a bright twelve-year-old girl! She is currently pursuing her MSc Marketing and is eager to share her story of discovery. Connect with Alison at:

alsionwatsonauthor@outlook.com

Transformation #13 - Samara Jacobs, Reading, UK

Samara Jacobs is a Shamanic Energy Medicine Practitioner and Woman of the Wild. Samara's commitment is to walk the Path of the Sacred, and as a Shaman, she talks about 'Being the Change' she wants to see in the World, which has led her down a path of Authenticity, balance, honesty and above all Beauty. Samara sees each moment

as an invitation to this commitment, stepping back into that place of vulnerability and humility, journeying with her elemental self and the Unity that this connection brings. She has set up her own business, which offers Shamanic Healing, as well as a connection back into the Natural World through Workshops she has personally created, based in Reading. Connect with Samara at:
www.wildwoodjourneys.co.uk

Transformation #14 - Carey Boyce, Sheffield, UK

Carey Boyce is a Kinesiologist, Energy Therapist and Motivational Coach and has worked in this field for over 25 years. In her work Carey teaches people how to calm their minds, boost their energy and brighten their mood in minutes. Her therapy business is 'How to be Happy in a Hurry', and she lives in Sheffield. Connect with Carey at:
www.howtobehappyinahurry.com

Transformation #15 - Theresa Fowler, London, UK

Theresa Fowler is a Self-Love and Weight Release Mentor, Speaker, Energetic Reflexologist and Author of self-published titles Feel Like Sh*t? How to Stop BEING Fat and upcoming self-love revolution manual Breakdowns to Breakthroughs: The 7 Secrets You Need to Know so you can Love Yourself. Through her own life experience and education, Theresa supports other women rebuilding their lives after burnout, so they reclaim their divine feminine wisdom, respect their bodies and re-energise their vitality and joy. Her passions also include running retreats and workshops for intelligent, like-minded women to connect and heal. Theresa spends her time between Rotterdam and London, England. Connect with Theresa at: www.theresamfowler.com

Transformation #16 - Natalie Bird, Manchester, UK

 Natalie believes that our past does not define us and that we can change ourselves and our planet for the better. Natalie coaches women to learn to trust themselves and their gut feeling so they can open up and trust again, following relationship breakdown. Natalie also helps women to understand their finances post relationship breakdown. Connect with Natalie at nataliebird@rocketmail.com

Transformation #17 - Annie Heggie, Woking, UK

 Annie, who recently retired, is a mother of 2, grandmother of 3. She is humble and enjoys life. Annie likes to spend time with her granddaughters, enjoys music especially Eric Clapton. She believes in angels and calls on Archangel Raphael who helps with her MS. Writing a book is on her to do list, so she is happy to be a contributor in Pivotal Moments 101. Connect with Annie at: annie.heggie@gmail.com

Transformation #19 - Alison Fennell, Merthyr Tydfil, UK

 Alison Fennell is a Welsh watercolour artist and instructor. She enjoys communicating the antics and nature of animals in her art and teaching adults the techniques of this chimerical medium. Now her focus is on connecting more deeply with nature for her wellbeing and for that of others and the planet. Over the last four years, Alison has produced as posters under license by John Lewis, Waitrose, and Dunelm who has sold her work UK wide. Alison has also been a contributing art tutor to Leisure Painter Magazine featuring articles for watercolour beginners." https://www.etsy.com/uk/shop/AlisonFennellArt

Transformation #20 - Zeleen Teter, Washington, USA

Zeleen is an Alaskan with a purpose. She was born in Anchorage, Alaska, the USA in the year 1978. Zeleen attended University of AK Anchorage, Baylor University, & American University in Washington, D.C. Zeleen has a taste for writing and has been published in a variety of magazines and has been an Assistant Editor for an issue of the Republican Party on Capitol Hill. She is also skilled in writing Press Releases. Keen on politics, Zeleen has attended Senate Hearings, met and spent time with someone who ran for President of the United States and a visitor to a range of embassies. Zeleen now spends time helping others with her unique gifts.

Transformation #21 - Bethany Rivett-Carnac, Bucks, UK

Bethany Rivett-Carnac is a love LED believer in the power of the heart and its capacity to light up the world. Passionate about the beauty and powerful transformation that comes from finding a balance between the masculine and feminine, she offers retreats, and group and private sessions that explore and awaken the divine blend that exists within us. Loving to illustrate love LED principles, you can find some of her Illustrations of Kindness in the Hay House published a book by the great Dr David Hamilton, entitled, 'The Five Side Effects of Kindness'. Connect with Bethany at: https://www.facebook.com/LoveLedCoaching/

Transformation #22 – Elizabeth Carney, Bucks, UK

Elizabeth Carney is a Master Coach and Healer. She is passionate about working with people to discover their authentic, true self so they can become fully visible as who they are meant to be. She has one son - the musician

Paddy James and lives in Hampshire with two crazy cats and a very bouncy Labrador. Connect with Elizabeth at:
Lizkelly1@me.com

Transformation #23 – Donegal, Ireland

 Emma is currently living in Paris, working as a Child Carer. She has spent the last year studying French and childcare, as well as becoming a qualified life coach, taking mental health, depression and burnout courses, along with studying the science of happiness. She is a writer and dreams of being an author, one day. This year, Emma will begin to study Psychology with counselling with Open University as she continues to live and work in Paris.
You can find her blog post, thoughts and musings at
https://www.facebook.com/
Half-Human-Half-Universe-1463855470591362/

Transformation #24 - Sarah Rossellini, Staffordshire, UK

 Sarah is a goal success coach. She inhales complex ideas and exhales simple truths; loves tall men and vertiginous heels. Science fiction/technology nerd, feminist, humanist, socialist, realist and ginger cat slave. Success goal: living on the beach; or on Mars; or ambitiously, a beach on Mars (must have Wi-Fi). You can contact Sarah at http://www.sarahrossellini.com

Transformation #25 - Amira Ben Mor, Kiryat Tivon, Israel

 Amira Ben Mordechai is a retired educator, headmistress, regional school supervisor and an author of many educational publications. Amira is active in an Arab-Jewish movement for a reformed equal rights society in Israel. She

has founded a Bridge card game club in her community with members typically of the elderly population, manages the club's website, has taught bridge and written a book for bridge learners. Amira is married, has two sons and a. daughter, eight lovely grandchildren, and two beautiful great-granddaughters Amira can be reached on Facebook at: https://www.facebook.com/amira.benmor

Transformation #26 - Roslyn Bell, Armagh, N. Ireland

Roslyn Bell described as a serial Entrepreneur with a multi-million-pound property empire is a survivor, inspirational speaker, business coach, advocate for women in business and author. Her message is one of courage, self-belief and determination to make it happen against all the odds. Connect with Roslyn at
www.roslynbell.com

Transformation #27 – Barbara Byrne, Dublin, Ireland

Barbara Byrne is passionate about Slimming World helping people lose weight and transform their lives. Helping change their thoughts to transform their world and achieve their weight loss dreams. She enjoys the outdoors, especially running and walking in nature. She also enjoys reading. Connect with Barbara at: Barbara.slimmingworld@ hotmail.com

Transformation #28 - Lucy Tobias, Buckinghamshire, UK

Lucy is a Shaman, Mentor and Coach. Having found her life purpose, she helps others live in their true authenticity, bringing their gifts and essence to the world. Her work enables her clients to transform their lives, facilitating

them to step into a new space, shining their light on the world. A life that is free from constraints, limiting beliefs and old stories. Her work is truly transformational. Lucy is looking forward to bringing the beautiful rites of the Munay Ki to the world 018. She lives in Buckinghamshire, UK, with her partner and two cats. She is a real lover of nature, the great outdoors and animals. Lucy has a passion for travel and learning about people and their cultures. Connect with Lucy at: **https://www.facebook.com/lucytshaman/**

Transformation #29 – Erron Noel, Colorado, USA

 Erron is an entrepreneur, speaker, author and a Divine Empowerment Coach. She is the Founder and Leader of "SHINE: The Movement". Daily she mentors aspiring and achieved enlightened leaders in mindset, personal power, and connection to The Divine. Erron connects their inner voice to the spiritual walk that will lead them to succeed in business and fulfilling relationships. Erron is the mother of two delightful daughters and enjoys the outdoors. Connect with Erron at: www. sherwoodenterprises.services4u.com

Transformation #30 - Debbie Arthurs, London, UK

 Debbie Arthurs works as a Freelance Holistic Therapist, and Counsellor. She also works alongside those with Dementia and Alzheimer's and believes strongly in the power of touch and being person-centred. A gentle hold of the hand connects both souls, in a calming and healing way. Debbie finds writing and art very cathartic; Debbie leads a full and happy life; there is life after a divorce! She describes herself as batty about dogs, music, nature, her friends and family. She can be found on Facebook and at: debbie@spirit-fire.co.uk

Transformation #31 - Jurgita Kasparr, London, UK

Jurgita Kasparr (Lithuanian) is a Transformational trainer and mentor. She knows how to unlock magical magnetic power in every woman, so her clients can claim her worth; attract success in personal life and business; experience what it means to be the woman who has it all without feeling guilty or being ashamed of own success. Jurgita is no stranger to writing and has already written an ebook, From Cinderella to Queen: 12 Ways to Become Irresistible to The Man You Want. Books play a big part in her life as she has been reading since she can remember. She enjoys dancing, swimming and driving at night. Jurgita is also a qualified image consultant and always has been interested in colour, clothes and how image affects people's lives.

Transformation #32 - Rita Grineviciene, London, UK

Rita Grineviciene is a 'Worth It' coach and author. She shows clients who they authentically are and how they ultimately deserve their dreams, as well as how to make them happen. Rita has two beautiful daughters. Rita came from Lithuania to the UK in 2007. Connect with Rita at www.empoweringquestions.co.uk

Transformation #33 - Brenda Dempsey, London, UK

See 'About the Creator'

Illustrator – Lacey Eshleman, Alaska, USA

 Lacey Eshleman Consciousness Coach, Artist, and Alchemist of life. She discovered through her own healing journey how connecting to our inner wisdom creates powerful shifts in mind, body, and spirit. It is her life's purpose to walk the talk and ignite the spark in others. Her bohemian nature has her in a constant state of rebirth, creating and connecting through her coaching practice and consciousness brand. She enjoys an inspired life that is constantly unfolding. Being a lifelong Alaskan has blessed her with many unique life experiences and continues to inspire her with the vastness of mother earth.

https://www.facebook.com/igniteconsciousness/
https://www.instagram.com/igniteconsciousness/
https://www.igniteconsciousness.com/

About the Creator

Brenda Dempsey (Domestic Abuse survivor, Catalyst and Problem Solver) is a Master Coach, Teacher, Mentor, Speaker and #1 International Best Selling Author. She is already published in the Anthology Book of Inspiration for Women by Women created by Australian Ruth Stuttgen and Conceived to Lead, Dismantling the Glass Ceiling Mindset created by American author Carla Wynn Hall. Coming soon her own work A-Z of Diamond Success. She has found a love of writing and uses this to assist other women in raising their voices with their own stories. She is the creator of Pivotal Moments 101 – An Anthological Trilogy full of transformational stories of Strength, Courage and Change Inspiring Hope in others written by women from around the globe.

Brenda believes that women can find their voice through writing and speak about their stories with a catalytic reaction of increasing their confidence, belief and courage to step into the spotlight and share their stories with other women illustrating their conviction to make a difference in the world today.

Through the book and work of Pivotal Moments 101, Brenda can realise her dream of bringing together women from around the globe as she creates a Retreat in Barbados in April 2018 followed by a global conference in Machu Picchu, Peru Summer 2018.

As a Transformational Coach, Brenda successfully empowers, inspires and uplifts women so they too can be free to live their life on their terms and achieve their dreams. Her vision is to create more leaders through the education and Diamond ripple effect of Holistic Leadership.

Brenda has founded a charity for Homeless women, focusing in their sanitary and hygiene, called Helping Handbags Worldwide. She is a mother of 4 smart kids and Grandmother to 7 beautiful grandchildren. Brenda loves to travel, with David her guardian angel, around the world leaving her mark on the lives of those she touches. She is a Scot who now lives in Surrey, UK.

Connect with Brenda at:

 Brendadempseydiamondsuccess

www.brendadempsey.co.uk

 @brendadempsey

hello@brendadempsey.co.uk

Lightning Source UK Ltd.
Milton Keynes UK
UKHW03f2047020418
320411UK00001B/36/P

9 781504 392204